18

6-2907
$2.⁰⁰
Sports

ONCE UPON A GAME

ONCE UPON A GAME

BASEBALL'S GREATEST MEMORIES

AS TOLD TO Alan Schwarz

HOUGHTON MIFFLIN COMPANY ◆ BOSTON NEW YORK 2007

For information about permission to reproduce
selections from this book, write to Permissions,
Houghton Mifflin Company, 215 Park Avenue South,
New York, New York 10003.

Visit our Web site: www.houghtonmifflinbooks.com.

Library of Congress Cataloging-in-Publication Data
Schwarz, Alan.
   Once upon a game : baseball's greatest memories /
as told to Alan Schwarz.
      p. cm.
   ISBN-13: 978-0-618-73127-5
   ISBN-10: 0-618-73127-X
   1. Baseball—United States—History—Miscellanea.
I. Title.
GV863.A1S39 2007
796.357'640973—dc22
2006030472

Book design by Lisa Diercks
The text of this book is set in Minion.

Printed in Singapore

TWP 10 9 8 7 6 5 4 3 2 1

Illustration Credits:
Courtesy of George F. Will: 11. AP/Chicago Tribune: 15. Getty:
1, 3, 7, 9, 16, 49, 51, 52, 61, 63, 64, 67, 103, 133, 138, 141, 142,
145, 146. Corbis: 1, 3, 8, 19, 20, 23, 25, 36, 47, 59, 72, 117, 118,
122, 150. Office of George H. W. Bush: 27. Yale University: 28.
Ron Vesely: 1, 3, 8, 9, 31, 68, 75, 99, 107, 121, 134. Boston Red
Sox: 7, 32. Universal City Studios: 7, 35. National Baseball Hall
of Fame: 7, 8, 9, 39, 40, 43, 44, 55, 83, 85, 87, 89, 92, 95, 96,
110, 111, 113, 114. AP: 56–57, 71, 100–101, 125, 127. Courtesy
of Dr. Charles Jeter: 76. Dan Arnold: 79. Stan Honda: 80. Don
Sparks/National Baseball Hall of Fame: 1, 91. Jerry Wachter:
104. John Klein: 108. *Sporting News*/Zuma Press: 129.
PEANUTS © United Feature Syndicate, Inc. Taken from the
June 9, 1967, *Peanuts* comic strip by Charles M. Schulz: 130.
Michael Zagaris: 149.

For Laura, because I want to

With the spirit of *Once Upon a Game* being the celebration of memories, Alan Schwarz and Houghton Mifflin Company are pleased to note that 20 percent of the author's royalties from sales of this book will be contributed to the Alzheimer's Association, the leader in Alzheimer's research and support. To preserve and protect our Memories from Alzheimer's disease, which afflicts an estimated 4.5 million Americans, join the cause:

Alzheimer's Association
225 N. Michigan Ave., 17th Floor
Chicago, IL 60601-7633
(800) 272-3900
www.alz.org

CONTENTS

ALAN SCHWARZ DIDN'T ASK ME FOR one of my most cherished baseball memories but I'm going to tell him anyway. It certainly has nothing to do with anything I accomplished on a baseball field. (My playing career, such as it was, took place in the uniform of the Mittendorf Funeral Home Panthers in the Champaign, Illinois, Little League, and ended in 1954, when I turned 13.) Rather high on my list—and it is a *long* list—of splendid memories is one from just before the top of the first inning of the Yankees-Orioles game in Baltimore's Camden Yards on the evening of September 20, 1998.

That was the night Cal Ripken, with no prior announcement, ended his playing streak at 2,632 consecutive games. I was there because Cal and Kelly had talked with me and my wife, Mari, about when and how to do this. They wanted to do it at home and without fuss.

When the Orioles took the field, and number 8 stayed in the dugout, Derek Jeter, the Yankee batting second that night, crouched in the on-deck circle and gave Cal a quizzical look. Yankee manager Joe Torre saw what was happening—that baseball history was being made—and, quietly gesturing with both hands,

he summoned his entire team to the top steps of the dugout. The first pitch was delayed while the entire Yankee team faced Cal and applauded. The home-plate umpire stood back and let the moment play out. Umpires, being baseball's judicial branch, are supposed to be dead to all human feeling, but they, too, understand the importance of baseball's institutional memory.

It might seem odd that of all the many major-league games I have seen, the vivid memory I choose to mention here involved neither a hit nor a pitch nor a catch nor a throw. It involved an act of sportsmanship in appreciation of baseball history. In appreciation, that is, of what Cal had done, and of what Lou Gehrig had done in setting the record that Cal had broken three seasons earlier. And in appreciation of the role of shared memories in the intergenerational transmission of affection for the game.

One of major-league baseball's durable strengths is that the game has a long history rich in such sparkling episodes. On July 4, 1876, America's centennial, the Chicago White Stockings lost to the Hartford Dark Blues, 3–0; and the Boston Red Caps, precursors to the Boston, then Milwaukee, then Atlanta Braves, defeated the St. Louis Brown Stockings, 4–3. Baseball has been generating memories a long time, and the sheer sweep of baseball's history, and fans' delight in conversation about comparisons between then and now, multiplies out memories. Why? Because the memories we have of players' achievements that we have seen are also, in a sense, memories of all the past achievements, spanning many generations, with which we compare contemporary events.

For example, when Ichiro Suzuki makes a spectacular throw, we are reminded of our memories—or of stories told to us—of throws by Roberto Clemente, just as when his throws thrilled fans, they were reminded of Tris Speaker's greatness. In baseball, the past is always present.

However, for many fans, the most lasting memories are often of the most mundane matters. Do you remember your first pair of real baseball shoes—ones with spikes? (My playing days were over before I got a league that permitted them.) Few people forget the first time they experienced the stunning sight of the green infield as they walked out of the city's gray concrete and into a ballpark. I will wager that many fans' most imperishable memory is of a voice over the radio—his or her team's play-by-play announcer calling a rare moment or repeating a trademark phrase.

Now, with this volume, we are given a new set of memories—those that the people featured in this book have shared with Alan Schwarz. And readers will find that these will refresh their own recollections. Baseball, like this book, is a gift that never stops giving.

—George F. Will
Washington, D.C., August 2006

11

THE BEST PART OF BEING A BASEBALL writer isn't writing. It's listening.

Any day I want, I can go to any ballpark, walk into the clubhouse, and talk with superstar and scrub alike about the games, the personalities, and the moments that all of us love to relive. Not just fans and writers. I've found that even though players are out there on the field performing, a part of them—like Tom Sawyer—is up in the balcony watching, appreciating the small role they're playing in the timeline of this wonderful sport. Listen carefully and you'll hear that they're fans, too.

This book is designed to let you pull up a chair with us and with every turn of the page listen in as some of baseball's greatest names recall their most personal memories. You'll hear Ernie Banks describe the first time he was moved to say, "Let's play two!" Roger Clemens remembers how he beat a traffic jam to strike out 20 Seattle Mariners one night in 1986. Gaylord Perry takes us back to the first game he won with a spitball, and Derek Jeter remembers the moment he realized he wanted to be a big-league ballplayer. How did Cal Ripken feel when he was just a struggling rookie? What was going through Bobby Thomson's mind before he hit the Shot Heard 'Round the World? What was it like for Terry Francona to be Michael Jordan's baseball manager?

Some of the best memories are from non-players—Kevin Costner describes the making of *Bull Durham* and *Field of Dreams,* and Charles Schulz, the late *Peanuts* cartoonist, shares why poor ol' Charlie Brown keeps losing games 40–0. George H. W. Bush takes us back to the day he shook hands with Babe Ruth. Every one of these vignettes comes from a personal interview with me—except a few, from long-deceased players, which come straight from old, long-forgotten articles I unearthed. Babe Ruth on his first home run as a 6-year-old? Casey Stengel on his first day in the big leagues? Those are simply too much fun to leave out.

From Yogi Berra to Curt Schilling, Nolan Ryan to Pedro Martinez, you should feel as if you're right there with me, listening to one great baseball storyteller after another. It's one big Ozzie Smith backflip. Speaking of which, turn to page 132.

—ALAN SCHWARZ
New York City, December 2006

12

ONCE UPON A GAME

ERNIE BANKS

No three words in the English language capture the joy of playing or watching baseball more than Ernie Banks's immortal line, "Let's play two!" From 1953 through 1971, Banks delighted fans not only with his amazing skills—he was one of the first power-hitting shortstops and wound up with 512 career home runs—but for his ever-present smile and elation at playing baseball for a living.

One afternoon in 1967, all those feelings came out in a battle cry that will live as long as baseball and hot dogs.

IT WAS TUESDAY, JULY 18, 1967—AT 10:25 A.M. Central Daylight Time. I know because it was one of the turning moments of my life.

I was driving down to Wrigley Field for our game against the Atlanta Braves. (It was a day game, of course—back then, all games at Wrigley were in the afternoon.) Sometimes I'd drive alongside Lake Michigan and relax mentally, but that day I went through some of Chicago's deprived communities just to remind myself how lucky and privileged I was to be a baseball player at beautiful Wrigley Field.

It was about 105 degrees that day, and as I walked into our locker room, my Cubs teammates were really worn down. But I was feeling so great. So lucky. I was getting paid to do something I loved. So I walked in the locker room and I said, "Boy, it's a beautiful day—let's play two!" Everybody kind of raised up and looked at me. They were saying to themselves, "This guy is crazy!"

"What are you talking about?" Billy Williams said. "It's 105 degrees out there and you're talking about playing two?"

"Yeah, let's play two today!"

I actually had almost said it a few weeks before. On July 2, we beat the Reds behind Fergie Jenkins 4–1 to move into a tie for first place. There were almost 40,000 people in Wrigley Field having such a great time. They raised the flag when we went into the tie for first place, and people were standing up and cheering. They didn't want to leave the park.

"I walked in the locker room and I said, "Boy, it's of raised up and looked at me. They were saying

ERNIE BANKS

a beautiful day—let's play two!" Everybody kind to themselves, "This guy is crazy!"

It was so joyful, I said to myself, "Boy, we should play two today." People just wanted to stick around and enjoy it forever. I saw from that day how much joy was in baseball and the social value of sports. It really uplifted the whole city. I was just amazed at that.

After I said, "Let's play two!" in the locker room, a writer in Chicago wrote about it, and it's really stuck to me ever since. I love it—it's become a part of me. It seems like athletes are remembered for just one thing. With Ted Williams, it's his .406 batting average. With Willie Mays, it's his over-the-shoulder catch. But people remember Ernie Banks for "Let's play two!"

More and more each day, I'm proud of that. It's become the benchmark of my life. I meet people now who were 10 or 12 years old when they came to Wrigley Field, and they say, "Ernie Banks! Let's play two!" Now those kids are running corporations and they tell me, "You always had all the joy for the game." It's just a wonderful thing and it's inspired my life all the way through up until now.

Baseball's the best game there is. My dad used to play catch with me growing up in Dallas because there was no high school team for me to play on. I was fortunate enough to play in exhibition games with Jackie Robinson, Roy Campanella, Larry Doby, and Don Newcombe when the Negro Leaguers did their barnstorming tours in the off-season. To watch all those guys, you couldn't help but say, "Wow, this is the greatest game!"

Pretty soon Buck O'Neil and the Kansas City Monarchs came through Dallas, and I got signed to play semipro ball in Amarillo, Texas. Then the Monarchs signed me up for good, and not long after that the Cubs got me. The rest is history.

I did a lot of things in my career on the field—500 home runs and everything—but the best part was sharing my joy for baseball with so many people. Every day of my life I wake up thinking, "Let's play two!" That will never change. ◆

17

ERNIE BANKS

No player won more World Series rings—10—than Yogi Berra, so it's easy to figure the Hall of Famer had been a can't-miss schoolboy player always destined for major-league stardom. That couldn't be further from the truth. Lawrence Peter "Lawdie" Berra grew up on the sandlots of St. Louis as a stocky, awkward runt of a kid who was told by the likes of Branch Rickey that he'd never make the major leagues. But proving his talent to the pros was nothing compared to convincing his skeptical immigrant father that signing a baseball contract was a better move than working for a living.

WHEN I WAS 14, I QUIT SCHOOL after the ninth grade and worked at a shoe factory to make some money for home. My family didn't want me playing baseball. My older brother Tony had the chance to sign a contract with the Cleveland Indians, but Pop wouldn't let him. He said Tony should work—and that's exactly what he told me, too.

But I couldn't be kept away from the ball field. Baseball was my life. It was everything I thought about all the time. I still remember going to work with a package wrapped in newspaper—everyone thought it was my lunch, but it was my baseball mitt. I would cut out

early to play with my friends. I just couldn't stay away from baseball.

I was always that way. I grew up in south St. Louis in an Italian neighborhood called the Hill. Joe Garagiola lived across the street from me. When we were 12, we and our friends formed a ball team we called the Stags. We would play against kids from the other side of town. We didn't have any real equipment or uniforms—just T-shirts. We'd always play harder against the teams with the nicer uniforms, which was most of the time!

Joe and I played every position back then—we just loved to play. (I was called Lawdie back then, because my mother had trouble

YOGI BERRA

"I couldn't be kept away from the ball field. Baseball was my life. It was everything I thought about all the time."

20

YOGI BERRA

saying Larry.) We'd play every day till it got dark. Then we'd go down to Riva's candy store for a soda or something. Joe and I got to be pretty good, mostly when we were playing for our local American Legion team.

(By the way, it was during my American Legion days that I got the nickname Yogi. We didn't have dugouts back then, so we would all just sit on the grass. I was kind of short and built funny, and when I sat there with my arms and legs crossed, one of the guys said, "You look like a yogi." That's when it happened.)

In 1941, when we were about 16, Joe and I went down to Sportsman's Park and got tried out by the St. Louis Cardinals and Branch Rickey. Mr. Rickey—that's what everyone in baseball called him—was known as a great judge of talent. He called me over after the tryout and said, "I don't think you'll ever be a big-league ballplayer, but you could be a good Triple-A player." I said, "Oh yeah?"

Joe was given a $500 bonus to sign, but they didn't offer me a contract. My best friend went off to play with our hometown Cardinals but I had to go back to work. I felt really bad about it. I wanted to prove I could play ball.

The next year, I got my chance. The Yankees gave me a tryout and asked what I wanted to sign. I demanded the same $500 Joe got,

and they said okay. But my father still didn't want me to go! Luckily, my brothers convinced Pop that I should be allowed to follow my dream. They said, "Dad, we're all working. Give Lawdie a chance to play." He finally gave in, and I became a professional ballplayer.

I played one season in the minors before being drafted into the navy. I was in the Normandy invasion—I served on a small boat that gave rocket cover to troops storming the coast of France. I went back to the minors in 1946 and was called up to the Yankees at the end of the year.

I walked into the clubhouse for the first time and couldn't believe my eyes. Charlie Keller, Tommy Henrich, Phil Rizzuto. Joe DiMaggio! All of those stars. It was great. A kid from the Hill going into a clubhouse like that?

In my second at-bat, I hit a home run. Boy, was I glad I wasn't back home in St. Louis working in that shoe factory. ◆

GEORGE BRETT

On July 24, 1983, George Brett hit one of the stickiest home runs in baseball history—the immortal Pine Tar Homer that no one who witnessed the scene will ever forget. With two out in the ninth against the Yankees, and facing the incomparable Goose Gossage, Brett smacked a two-run home run to give the Royals a 5–4 lead. But Yankees manager Billy Martin had other ideas . . .

LET ME SET THE SCENE FOR YOU. I'M playing for the Royals, against our archrival at the time, the Yankees. I hit a two-out home run against one of the toughest relievers ever, Goose Gossage, to give us the lead. I jog around the bases and take my seat in the dugout, feeling pretty good about myself.

All of a sudden the umpires are looking at my bat. Something about the pine tar on it. It might have too much? You gotta be kidding. Who cares? But they kept talking and looking at my bat. I remember sitting on the bench saying to myself, "If they call me out, *I'm gonna kill one of those guys!*"

Next thing I know, they do just that, and I'm sprinting out of the dugout completely berserk. The video of me now is pretty hilarious, with me charging the umps, having to be held back, yelling and screaming and flailing my arms, but at the time it wasn't funny. It was highway robbery!

It was no secret that I'd always used a lot of pine tar on my bat. I didn't wear batting gloves—I liked the feel of my skin on the wood. I would put the pine tar up higher on the bat and just rub it when I needed some for a better grip. Technically it was against the rules—you couldn't put pine tar more than 18 inches up the handle—and umpires told me to clean up my bat from time to time, but no one really worried about it.

Two weeks before the Pine Tar Game, when we were playing the Yankees in Kansas City, Billy Martin noticed I had pine tar too far up the bat. But being the competitor Billy was, he didn't say anything then. He wanted to wait until I did something to beat them

GEORGE BRETT

and then get it disallowed. His chance came when I hit that two-out homer against the Goose. Did the pine tar help me hit the homer? Of course not! I hit the ball 29 inches up the handle. The ball wasn't close enough to the pine tar to smell it.

But the umpires agreed with Billy that it was an illegal bat, so *bam*—I was out. And worse, the game was over. We'd lost, 4–3. I was furious, as the video lives on to prove. (Most people forget that during all the mayhem, Gaylord Perry—one of our pitchers who was known to, um, bend the rules a bit—was trying to get the bat to the clubhouse and hide the evidence.) They finally calmed me down, and we left New York that night. But boy, was I still steamed.

Luckily, the American League president, Lee MacPhail, realized during our protest of the game over the next few weeks that us losing on such a technicality was really unfair. He ordered that my home run count and that on August 18 we resume the game with the Royals leading 5–4. It was such a happening in New York that the Yankees tried to charge regular admission just to see those last four outs!

Billy Martin was so mad that he played Ron Guidry (his best pitcher) in center field and Don Mattingly (a left-handed first baseman) at second base. When the Yankees came to bat in the bottom of the ninth, our ace reliever, Dan Quisenberry, retired the Yankees in order. Royals win, 5–4! After almost a whole month, the game was finally over.

Honestly, the whole Pine Tar mess was the best thing that ever happened to me in my career. In 1980, I had to miss a couple of innings of a World Series game because of a whopping case of hemorrhoids. For the next three years all I heard from fans were Preparation H jokes. But after the Pine Tar Game I wasn't the Hemorrhoid Guy anymore. I was the Pine Tar Guy. Who would you rather be known as?

I still get a laugh out of the Pine Tar Game. Whenever my oldest son, Jackson, was bored, he'd always ask me the same thing. "Dad," he'd say, "can we put in that tape where you get real mad?" ◆

24

"I remember sitting on the bench saying to myself, 'If they call me out, **I'm gonna kill one of those guys!'"**

GEORGE BRETT

Many presidents pretend to be baseball fans, but George H. W. Bush adored the game like perhaps none before or since. He led Yale to the College World Series two years in a row, in 1947 and 1948, as a slick-fielding first baseman, and as president kept his trusty first-sacker's mitt in his White House desk drawer. (He also made sure that, should he ever find himself in a presidential jam, a bookshelf outside the Oval Office always had a copy of *The Baseball Encyclopedia*.) Every now and then he'd sift through that book and land on the page detailing the great Babe Ruth, whom Bush had met as a young Yalie some 40 years before.

I'VE MET A LOT OF FAMOUS PEOPLE IN my lifetime: world leaders, Nobel Prize–winning scientists, heroes and villains alike. But nothing compares to the afternoon in June 1948 when I met the one and only Babe Ruth.

I was the senior captain of the Yale University baseball team at that time—a first baseman who didn't hit much but was pretty good defensively. Before a big game against Princeton at Yale Field, the Babe was on hand for a special ceremony. He was donating his personal manuscript of his autobiography, *The Babe Ruth Story,* to the Yale library. I got to represent my team on the field with him

and couldn't believe that I was out there with Babe Ruth himself.

He wasn't quite the Babe Ruth I'd been a fan of for most of my young life. Cancer had its grip on him pretty bad—he was all hunched over and could barely speak. His hand was trembling when he handed the manuscript to me. But he was still the Babe.

He leaned over and croaked, "You know, when you write a book like this, you can't put *everything* in it."

I was overwhelmed. I had been a Babe fan ever since my dad took us to the ballpark when we were kids. I had been more of a Red Sox fan back in those days, but Ruth was

"Even as a dying man—he passed away a few months after that day—he had a tremendous, commanding presence."

everybody's hero. Even as a dying man—he passed away a few months after that day at Yale Field—he had a tremendous, commanding presence. You wanted to see him grab a bat and swat a couple out of the ballpark.

It was sad to see him in that state, but getting to meet him was one of the highlights of my life. He was still the icon. He was still The Man.

You da man, Babe. ◆

ROGER CLEMENS

ON HIS FIRST 20-STRIKEOUT MASTERPIECE

The baseball world had barely heard of Roger Clemens when he took the mound against the Mariners on April 29, 1986. Three hours later, no one would ever forget him.

Still an unproven 23-year-old coming off shoulder surgery, Clemens struck out 20 Seattle Mariners to top the major-league record held by three Hall of Famers: Tom Seaver, Nolan Ryan, and Steve Carlton. Before more than 300 lifetime victories, before seven Cy Young Awards and countless exceptional performances, Clemens's own legend began that night at Fenway Park—that is, only after a wicked traffic jam that almost cost him that start in the first place . . .

THERE ARE SOME NIGHTS WHEN YOU just know you're going to pitch great. But this was not one of those nights. At first, I was worried I wouldn't pitch at all.

I was caught in traffic on Storrow Drive on my way to Fenway Park. You wouldn't believe how jammed it was—the game started at 7:35, I usually get to the ballpark two hours before the game, and at 5:35 I'm still stuck in gridlock. I don't move for an hour. Now I'm sweating—I can see the CITGO sign up above Fenway and we're not moving. Sitting next to me is my wife, Deb, and I tell her that I'm gonna run the two miles to the ballpark. As I'm changing from boots into sneakers out-side my car a motorcycle officer pulls up and is about to ask me what in the world I'm doing when he says, "Hey, aren't you . . .?"

"Uh, yeah."

"Aren't you pitching tonight?"

"Yeah."

"Follow me."

He split the sea of traffic for us, and when I got to Fenway at 6:58, I was so sweaty and nervous it looked like I'd already warmed up. My pitching coach asked if I wanted to just go the next day, but I said I was fine. I dressed as fast as Superman in a phone booth, rushed to the bullpen, and got ready. I'm not sure I threw two strikes in 30 warm-up pitches.

30

Of course that changed during the game. I struck out the side in the first inning and started to feel good, especially on what was a pretty cold April night. I whiffed 11 more in the next five innings on almost all fastballs—I didn't throw more than 20 breaking balls all night. I started to think that I was getting a lot of strikeouts, but I had bigger problems. It was still a scoreless game.

And then I was losing. After two more strikeouts in the seventh, Gorman Thomas, a pretty darned good power hitter, smacked a fastball over the Green Monster to put the Mariners ahead, 1–0. When I got back to the dugout I whipped my glove down, walked back to the Sox clubhouse, and kicked a chair over. I was mad because I had started getting into strikeout mode instead of pitching smart, and it had cost me.

Thank goodness things turned around

quickly. Dwight Evans hit a clutch two-out, three-run homer in the bottom of the seventh to give us a 3–1 lead, and I got really pumped up. I struck out two more in the eighth to give me 18 K's. I could tell something special was happening because my teammates started to not talk to me and not sit next to me, like I was throwing a no-hitter or something. I had no idea that I was getting close to the strike-out record of 19 when I went back to the clubhouse after the eighth to change my shirt. My pitching teammate Al Nipper followed me up there.

back to full strength. But this night was showing what I was still capable of. That, I knew.

In the ninth, I struck out Spike Owen for No. 19, and then threw a two-strike fastball to Phil Bradley. He took it. The umpire's hand went up—strike three, No. 20. The Fenway crowd just went crazy, and I have to admit my heart was pumping pretty good, too. I could have gotten another strikeout for No. 21, but Ken Phelps grounded out. We won 3–1, and I had done something no other pitcher had ever done—20 strikeouts in a nine-inning game, and not one walk, either.

"I had no idea that I was getting close to the strike-out record of 19 when I went back to the clubhouse after the eighth."

"I gotta tell you," he said, "because I'm pretty sure you don't know. You need two strikeouts for a major-league record."

I just looked at him. I had great control that night—I didn't walk anyone—and just kept my concentration on battling the hitters. People forget that before that night I had been hurt. My shoulder had been operated on the year before, and no one knew if I'd ever make it

I'm not positive, but I'm pretty sure Bruce Hurst gave me my nickname that night: The Rocket. I got so many calls afterward, up until four that morning. President Ronald Reagan called. So did his V.P., George Bush. My old teammates at the University of Texas called, thinking that the 20 strikeouts in the box score was a misprint. I couldn't help but say out loud to them, "I'm in the Hall of Fame!" ◆

KEVIN COSTNER

No other actor in the history of American film has left a more indelible imprint on baseball movies than Kevin Costner. As Crash Davis in 1988's *Bull Durham,* **he captured the tricks and trials of a now-legendary minor-league journeyman. The next year, in** *Field of Dreams,* **he made an Iowa cornfield a symbol of America's rural pastime. He capped off the trilogy in 1999 with the fittingly titled** *For Love of the Game.*

The best part of Costner's baseball movies is that he isn't altogether acting. Costner has been an avid fan all his life, and he enjoys sharing stories of playing baseball in the streets as a kid, his favorite movie scenes, and even the best scenes that no one ever saw.

I REMEMBER EVERYTHING ABOUT PLAYing baseball as a kid. I pitched three or four no-hitters in Little League. But I loved playing in the street just as much. I can remember looking for beer cartons to make second base. Sliding in the street just because you wanted to be safe. I remember how you chose teams, and the kids' faces. I remember getting in trouble when my dad had to come get me when I was late for dinner—I was in so much trouble. I remember watching a car come down the street and yelling, "C'mon, we can get one more play in. Just pitch it!"

So much of *Field of Dreams* has to do with a grown man's relationship with his father, connecting to baseball through his dad. That's where I learned the game, too. My dad coached Little League. In the opening montage of *For Love of the Game,* all the pictures are of me and my father. (My little dog's in there too.) I became such a fan of major-league players that I once built a canoe and put *Sports Illustrated* covers all over it. I thought, "How cool, man." But it just looked so stupid. I don't know what I was thinking.

I played baseball up through high school and even thought about trying out for my college team at Cal State Fullerton, but I didn't

KEVIN COSTNER

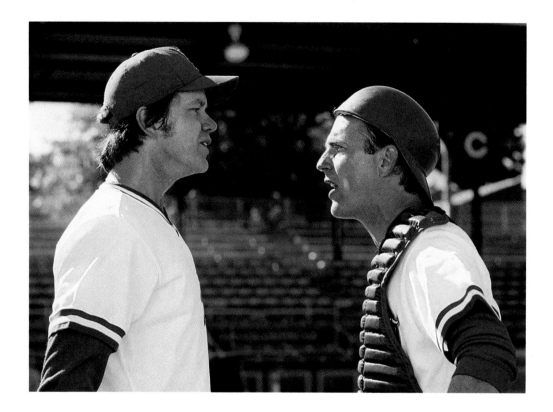

end up doing it. I became an actor and stayed connected to baseball through the characters I played.

People think that filming baseball movies is like playing, just horsing around on the field, but it can be pretty rough. We shot *Bull Durham* at old Durham Athletic Park in the off-season, usually late at night or early in the morning, and it was freezing. (If you look carefully, you can see the breath coming out of Tim Robbins's and my mouths on the mound.) And the scene outside the bar, when I'm daring Nuke LaLoosh (played by Tim) to throw a fastball right at me? It was pretty scary, because Tim was erratic—both his character and him. He missed me by a good three feet, thank goodness, but I swear when I was standing there I thought, "I gotta play

KEVIN COSTNER

this thing like a hero, but I could end up with a mouthful of ball."

To shoot *For Love of the Game*, I had to throw 100 pitches five days in a row—and I'd hurt my arm on the first day. But I still went out there to the Yankee Stadium mound to pitch. After a while, I couldn't throw anymore from the pain up and down my arm. I went when the team cut Crash at the end and he went wandering through the night. This is before he ends up on the porch with Annie, Susan Sarandon's character. Crash wanders in the night and he comes up on these old black guys who are drinking wine, just sitting there on Main Street, one of these little towns in America. He kind of stumbles into them, and

"People think that filming baseball movies is like playing, just horsing around on the field, but it can be pretty rough."

back to the dugout and . . . well, not to be too graphic about it, I threw up, right there in the legendary Yankee Stadium dugout. At least I had the good manners to not do it on the mound in front of everybody.

People ask me what my favorite scenes are from *Field of Dreams*. I like when my character tells Dr. Graham, "Oh my God, you can't go back. I'm sorry." And I liked him asking his father, "Hey, Dad, you wanna have a catch?" I think everyone loves that.

As for my favorite scene from *Bull Durham*, it got cut—so no one ever saw it. It was before long you see they're rolling up papers into balls and pitching to him, sharing a bottle of wine. They were just pitching to him. Crash is there just launching these paper balls. And you saw how difficult it was for him to let go.

I understood that lonely quality. I can't let baseball go either. ◆

DOM DiMAGGIO

Everyone knows that Joe DiMaggio holds the major-league record for hitting in 56 straight games, but few remember that his younger brother, Dominic, still owns the Red Sox team record of 34. Nicknamed the Little Professor, Dom scorched the ball throughout the summer of 1949 as his Red Sox and Joe's Yankees mounted what might have been their most exciting race ever for the American League pennant.

A LOT OF PEOPLE MAKE A BIG DEAL about my 34-game hitting streak in the summer of 1949, and how it was snapped on a great play in center field by my brother Joe. I'd like to set the record straight.

First of all, when I hit in 34 games in a row, I was only doing my job. I played every game pretty much as I played any other game. I got my fair share of walks during the streak—I don't think I chased bad pitches. I was a line-drive hitter. My job was to get on base and let the sluggers like Ted Williams drive me home. I wasn't even aware of my streak until it was at 22 or 23 games, and I didn't make a big deal of it.

On the day it ended, August 9, we were playing the Yankees at Fenway Park. Our rivalry with the Yankees was great—every bit as emotional as it is now. The atmosphere was very thick whether we played at Fenway Park or Yankee Stadium. That afternoon we were in third place, six games behind the first-place Yankees, but playing great. We were just entering the pennant race. These were big games.

But when you feel pressure, you do not perform. The first thing you've got to do is be completely relaxed. And that's the way I was. On that day against the Yankees, I felt good. I hit one solid shot to the third baseman that was turned into an out. I got out another couple of times. I was 0-for-4 when I got to the plate in the eighth inning against Vic Raschi, who was a darn good pitcher.

I smacked a line drive right up the middle so hard that it passed Raschi's ear! He ducked to get out of the way of it! As soon as I hit it, I said, "Okay, that's 35." But that ball wouldn't drop. The ball refused to drop. Joe is standing

Dom DiMaggio (*right*) with big brother, Joe.

DOM DIMAGGIO

"The only statistic that really matters to me **is hitting .300.**"

out there in center field, and he didn't have to move. He said it himself later—if he hadn't caught the ball, it would have hit him right between the eyes. So there was no effort on his part. It wasn't a great play by him, like they're still saying today. I just hit the ball too damn hard!

But the streak was over, and I didn't mind that much. (After all, we'd won the game, 6–3.) And hitting streaks didn't matter to me, even when I hit in another 27 straight in 1951. It's just a statistic. And the only statistic that really matters to me is hitting .300. I did it four times in my 10 full seasons in the major leagues, and finished with a .298 average lifetime. My only regret is not reaching .300.

It would have meant so much. Enos Slaughter hit exactly .300 in his career—and he's in the Hall of Fame. Why? Did he hustle any more than I did? Did he have a better arm than I did? Did he run the bases any better than I did? Did he play defense as well as I did? Who knows? All I needed was 12 more hits—only about one per season—and I would have had a .300 average.

But that's okay. As I said, I was a leadoff man. I think one of the finest compliments paid to me was from my own teammate Bobby Doerr. He said to me on more than one occasion, "Dommy, if you had been batting fifth or sixth in the lineup, I am positive you would drive in 100 runs a year." That to me was the ultimate compliment. Just like the streak, I did what my job called for. ◆

Bob Feller was the greatest teenage pitcher baseball has ever seen. Starting out with the Cleveland Indians at age 17—before even finishing high school back in tiny Van Meter, Iowa—Rapid Robert and his 100-mph fastball became the greatest strikeout sensation in the American League, and he was quickly becoming perhaps the best pitcher in the history of baseball.

But Feller gave it all up after the 1941 season to serve in the U.S. Navy, not knowing if he would ever return to the major leagues.

I WAS DRIVING MY NEW BUICK CENTURY across the Mississippi River, across the Iowa-Illinois state line, when my world —everyone's world—changed forever.

It was December 7, 1941. I was driving to a meeting with my Cleveland Indians bosses to hash out my 1942 contract, and out it came on the radio: The Japanese had bombed Pearl Harbor.

The last thing on my mind right then was playing baseball. I immediately decided to enlist in the U.S. Navy. I didn't have to—I was 23 and strong-bodied, you bet, but with my father terminally ill back in Van Meter, I was exempt from military service. It didn't matter to me—I wanted to join the fight against Hitler and the Japanese. We were losing that war, and most young men of my generation wanted to help push them back. People today don't understand, but that's the way we felt in those days. We wanted to join the fighting. So on December 9, I gave up the chance to earn $100,000 with the Indians and became the first professional athlete to join the navy after Pearl Harbor.

It was one of the greatest experiences in my life. You can talk about teamwork on a baseball team, but I'll tell you, it takes teamwork when you have 2,900 men stationed on the USS *Alabama* in the South Pacific. I was a chief petty officer. I helped give exercises and ran the baseball team and recreation when we were in port. But I was also a gun captain—I was firing a 40-millimeter quad at eight rounds per second.

42

"Had I not
missed
those
almost four
seasons
to World
War II . . .
I might
have had
370 or even
400 wins.
But I have
no regrets.
None at
all."

BOB FELLER

The *Alabama* was involved in one of the most important battles of the Pacific. In June 1944, we were supposed to shell the beaches of Saipan for two hours so that our marines could land safely. The Japanese tried a surprise attack—but we were ready. The U.S. Navy and Air Force, we had all the big carriers and battleships like the *Iowa*, the *Wisconsin*, the *New Jersey*, the *Alabama*; you name it, we had them all. Our pilots and gunners shot down 474 Japanese aircraft, sunk three of their carriers, and got several of their escort ships. And when the sun went down that night, it was the end of the Japanese naval air force. We made it look so easy, ever since they've called it the Great Marianas Turkey Shoot.

We were involved in so many other important engagements, including some in the North Atlantic over in Europe. Our ship won nine battle stars, eight of them while I was on it. It was an incredible time for all of us.

I went on inactive duty in August 1945, and since I had stayed in such good shape and had played ball on military teams, I was ready to start for the Indians just two days later, against the Tigers. More than 46,000 people came to see me return—there was such a patriotic feeling, with V-J Day so fresh in everyone's minds. Even though I hadn't pitched in the major leagues in almost four years, I struck out the first batter. I wound up throwing a four-hitter and winning 4–2. What a great night . . . I kept it up the rest of the season, too, and then had what many people call my best season in 1946, when I won 26 games with 348 strikeouts.

A lot of folks say that had I not missed those almost four seasons to World War II—during what was probably my physical prime—I might have had 370 or even 400 wins. But I have no regrets. None at all. I did what any American could and should do: serve his country in its time of need. The world's time of need.

I knew then, and I know today, that winning World War II was the most important thing to happen to this country in the last 100 years. I'm just glad I was a part of it. I was a gun captain on the battleship *Alabama* for only 34 months. People have called me a hero for that, but I'll tell you this—heroes don't come home. Survivors come home. ◆

In the winter of 1994, a few months after he retired from basketball to grieve over the death of his father, Michael Jordan decided to pursue a lifelong dream—to become a major-league baseball player.

Most people mocked him—he hadn't played baseball since high school back in North Carolina—but Jordan reported to the Class AA Birmingham Barons, where a young manager named Terry Francona was assigned to teach the most famous athlete in the world how to hit a breaking ball. Francona later led the Boston Red Sox to the 2004 World Series championship, ending 86 years of Hub heartbreak, yet he will also forever be remembered as Michael Jordan's minor-league skipper.

NOT A LOT OF MINOR-LEAGUE MANagers are too happy when their right fielder hits .202 with three home runs the entire season. But not many minor-league managers—in fact, I'm the only one—ever got to manage Michael Jordan.

It was a blast. Not because I was around the greatest basketball player who ever lived. I was managing a really dedicated athlete, someone who cared deeply about working at a game he loved. Here was a guy who'd been making a gazillion dollars a year, and he gave it up to ride buses in the Southern League with the Birmingham Barons. And you know what? He might have been the most respectful player on that team. He listened to instruction and learned all the lingo. He loved being treated as just a regular farmhand. He stayed at the same motels as the rest of us, rode on the same bus, played Yahtzee with the guys. And I'll tell you something—he could play baseball a bit too.

People gave Michael a hard time that he hit only .202, but give the guy a break—he hadn't played baseball competitively in 15 years, since high school! I think he did amazingly well considering that. Hitting a baseball is the hardest thing to do in sports, and the Southern League is a tough, tough league. I honestly believe that had Michael gotten another two years of breaking balls under his belt, with his

dedication, he could have made it to the major leagues as a fourth or fifth outfielder. He wouldn't have accepted anything less.

Michael did have some raw moments on the baseball field, that's for sure. And not just because his swing was a little long. Early on he stole third base a couple of times when we were leading by like 10 runs. The other dugout got pretty steamed. I'd tell him, "Hey, M.J., uh . . ." and he just didn't understand. His response was, "Hey, they give you a lay-up, you take it!" When we fined him like $25 in kangaroo court for missing a bunt or something, he gladly paid up.

He was a decent player. I know it was fashionable to bash him, but I spent the whole year with M.J. and saw him play firsthand. I'm telling you, there is nothing there to bash. This guy was legit. He hit three home runs, and they were legitimate homers. He stole 30 bases. He had a decent arm, and he could go left to right in the outfield about as well as anyone I saw. I really do wish he could have stuck with it. But he decided the next spring to go back to the NBA, which of course I understood.

Michael called me on the way to the arena one day after that. He said, "I just wanted to tell you I love doing what I do again." He'd gotten tired of basketball, and baseball was just so joyful for him. "You guys love what you do," he said, "and that rubbed off on me." I truly think that getting a hit in an important part of the game for the Birmingham Barons meant as much to him that year as any jump shot in the NBA.

Not that Michael could stay away from basketball for a whole year. During the Arizona Fall League that October a bunch of guys and him went to a gym in Scottsdale for a pickup game. It was awesome. Man, was he competitive. He hated to lose, even in a meaningless game like that.

I'll never forget one game. Michael was on my team—I was the boss, after all!—and I was out of gas near the end. I took the last shot, missed badly, and we lost. I didn't care. But Michael came up to me as we were walking off.

"I always shoot last."

"Huh?" I said.

"I always shoot last."

"On TV you do."

"I *always* shoot last."

He was serious! He was actually kind of ticked off. So I yelled at him as he was walking away: "Now you know how I feel when you try to hit the curveball!"

He got about two more steps before he just fell to the floor laughing. For that one year with the Birmingham Barons, Michael Jordan was just one of the guys. ◆

"I honestly believe that had Michael gotten another two years of breaking balls under his belt, with his dedication, he could have made it to the major leagues as a fourth or fifth outfielder."

TERRY FRANCONA

NOMAR GARCIAPARRA

All-Star slugger Nomar Garciaparra is a bundle of superstitious quirks. He taps his toes at the plate to make sure his shoes are tight. He tugs at his batting gloves. He always descends into the dugout one step at a time, touching each step with both feet. One of his most famous routines is to always place his glove, ever so gently, on the same spot on the dugout bench. Most people have no idea why he does this. The ritual dates all the way back to his boyhood in California, when his father gave him the gift of a lifetime.

IT WAS MY SECOND YEAR IN T-BALL, when I was 6 years old. My dad (Ramon, which he spelled backward to invent my unique name) bought me a baseball mitt. It wasn't cheap. It was a Mizuno professional model and cost about $125.

We had no money to spare, by any means. We weren't poor—we had what we needed—but $125 for a baseball glove? My father gave it to me because I loved the game, and he knew I'd take care of it. And I did. I treasured that glove. I didn't want anyone to use it. If some kid picked it up and threw it, I got really mad. And when I came off the field after an inning, I never tossed my glove into the dugout. I placed it down on the bench. It was a respect for my equipment. Even when I was

that young, I knew how special it was for my dad to do something like that for me. I didn't want to disappoint him. I guess I honor that to this day by still treating my glove just like I did when I was a kid.

I was always a serious kid when it came to baseball. During practice I was really focused on learning. I wasn't out there jumping around, I wasn't chasing butterflies. I was really in tune with the game. I used to have this stern look on my face as a little kid. It must have been pretty funny. I remember one year, every kid on the team got a trophy. And on my trophy they called me "No-Nonsense Nomar."

I have plenty of fun on the field, but I'll always remember how hard it was to work my way up to the major leagues. I wasn't a special

NOMAR GARCIAPARRA

"It's kind of a bummer that **I can't use the glove my dad bought me** back when I was 6."

ballplayer as a kid. I was short and skinny, no different from everyone else. It wasn't, "Oh my God, this guy's gonna be something. He's gonna make it." But I always said I was going to be a major-league ballplayer, because that's what I loved more than anything else. I was dead set on making it come true.

It's kind of a bummer that I can't use the glove my dad bought me back when I was 6. I used it up to high school. I used it for so long, there was no padding left in it. So I had to get another one. But I'll never forget it. I could win a dozen Gold Gloves in the major leagues, and none of them will be more special than that old Mizuno. ◆

It's hard to appreciate today what Hank Greenberg meant to the Jewish population of the United States during the 1930s and 1940s. As Hitler rampaged through Europe, and anti-Semitism challenged Jews' dignity at home, Greenberg—a hulk of a man at 6 foot 4 and 215 pounds—seemed to put all their dreams for respect on his immense shoulders as he slugged his way to national celebrity, all the while being openly taunted as "kike" and "Jewboy" by opposing players.

In the years before he died in 1986, at the urging of his son, Steve, Hank Greenberg spent hours sitting by his pool in Beverly Hills, California, speaking into a tape recorder so the memories of his career and personal challenges could be preserved. Below is his account of the most remarkable moment in his most remarkable career: his grand slam on the final day of the 1945 season, just months after returning from four years in the U.S. Army, to win the American League pennant for Detroit.

WE WENT INTO ST. LOUIS LEADing Washington by one game and needing a win in the final two games to clinch the pennant. For three straight days, games were rained out. On September 30 a double-header was scheduled. The commissioner wanted the games played, otherwise we would win the pennant by default. Of course, he wanted it won or lost on the field.

The Browns were in third place and had been playing well. If we lost both games, we'd end up in a tie with the Senators. They had concluded their season and had assembled in their clubhouse, all packed and ready to go, to listen to our ball game on the radio. Their best pitcher, Dutch Leonard, had been sent to Detroit to rest up for a playoff game in the event we lost to the Browns.

I hated Washington. They had played a lot of dirty tricks on me over the years, like Jake Powell running into me for no reason at all

54

and breaking my wrist, and their catcher telling Jimmie Foxx of the Philadelphia Athletics the pitches so he could tie me for the 1935 league home-run title. (In 1984, 49 years later, I got a letter from a friend who had been a substitute player for the Senators in 1937, and he told me that the Washington catcher was telling Foxx what pitches were coming up. After the game, the catcher was bragging about how he managed to keep me from leading the league in home runs. The pitcher hadn't been aware during the game that his own catcher was giving signs away to the enemy, and when he heard about it, he walked up and punched the catcher in the nose.)

It rained all day the day of the game. The game was delayed for 50 minutes. By the time the game began, there weren't many people at the ballpark.

Rain fell throughout the game. The Browns were beating us 3–2 when we came to the top of the ninth. The afternoon light was now very dim. The umpires didn't want to call the game, though, because the pennant was at stake.

The first man up for us was Hub Walker, pinch-hitting for Hal Newhouser. Hub singled. Then Skeeter Webb bunted him over. The throw went to second base and it hit Walker, putting men on first and second. Then Eddie Mayo laid down another bunt for us, and he sacrificed. Now there were men on second and third. Doc Cramer, a left-handed batter, came to bat, and the Browns, who had a right-handed pitcher on the mound, Nelson Potter, decided to walk him.

So the bases were full. That brought me to the plate.

The Browns had loaded the bases to pitch to me because they were hoping that I would hit into a double play. The rain continued to

fall. I took the first pitch from Nelson Potter for a ball. As he wound up on the next pitch, I could read his grip on the ball and I could tell he was going to throw a screwball. I swung and hit a line drive toward the corner of the left-field bleachers. I stood at the plate and watched the ball for fear the umpire would call it foul. It landed a few feet inside the foul pole for a grand slam.

We won the game and the pennant, and all the players charged the field when I reached home plate and they pounded me on the back and carried on like I was a hero. Because of the rain there was almost nobody in the stands to pay attention, and there were few newspapermen. Just the ballplayers giving me a hero's welcome.

When we returned to Detroit there were thousands of people in the train station giving me a big hand. But the best part of that home run was hearing later what the Washington players said: "God damn that dirty Jew bastard, he beat us again." They called me all kinds of names behind my back, and now they had to pack up and go home while we went to the World Series. ◆

"After the game, the catcher was bragging about how he managed to keep me from leading the league in home runs."

ON GOING DEEP WITH HIS FATHER

One of baseball's most idyllic images is that of fathers playing catch with sons. But on September 14, 1990, one father-and-son pair did something none had done before or has matched since.

Playing together with the Seattle Mariners, Ken Griffey Sr. and Jr. hit back-to-back home runs. For the serious veteran and his fun-loving oldest boy, the moment became a bonding of two generations that the baseball world reveled in with them. Ken Griffey Jr. went on to hit more than 500 home runs afterward, but to him, none was more meaningful.

I**T HAPPENED REAL QUICK.** I'd seen my father hit home runs so many times. But I'd never been able to hit one right afterward—playing on the same team, in the same lineup, back-to-back. Father and son. Senior and Junior. This was the chance any son would dream of.

My dad played in the major leagues for most of my childhood. He was always with the Reds or the Yankees or the Braves while I was growing up, and he didn't get to see me play that much. I understood, but it still was kind of a bummer. So when he signed with the Mariners late in the 1990 season, when I was finishing up my second full year in the majors, I couldn't believe I finally had a chance to spend so much time with my dad.

It was great just to see him out there and play the game we both love and to have someone around where I knew that no matter what happened he was 100 percent behind me. He loved it too. He said to me when we started, "We're going to have fun for six weeks —this is the best thing that's ever happened to me." That's exactly what he told me.

Dad was 40 at the time, just winding down his career, and I told him, "Dad, you protected me for 20 years, so now I'm gonna protect you." He hit second and I hit third, but he didn't need any help from me. In his first nine games he batted .484! The next game we played was against the Angels in Anaheim, and the script couldn't have been cooler if they'd done it up the road in Hollywood.

KEN GRIFFEY JR.

KEN GRIFFEY JR.

In the top of the first inning, Dad tattooed an 0-2 pitch 20 feet over the center-field wall. Just crushed it. I was so happy for him. He ran around the bases, touched home plate, and I was there to congratulate him. He just said, "That's how you do it, son." I looked back at him and accepted his challenge.

I worked a 3-0 count, and even though I was a young player, I got the green light from the dugout to swing if I wanted to. The next pitch was close to my wheelhouse so I just let 'er rip. I got ahold of it and shot it to left field on the line. It kept going and going . . . and finally dropped over the fence.

I was kind of laughing as I went around the bases because I wanted to share the moment with my dad. My teammates started coming out of the dugout to congratulate me —but my dad was nowhere to be found! He was hiding! Actually, he was still on the bench, making sure that I shook everyone else's hand before I shook his. But when I finally got to him, it was worth the wait. He gave me a hug and said, "We did it."

It didn't take long for us to do a little trash-talking. I told him, "Mine got out quicker." And he responded, cool as he always is, "Yeah, only because it didn't go as far!"

Later that night, we got to talking about the incredible moment—one that's definitely up there with all the moments I've had as a ballplayer. He looked at me and said, "Do you realize what we did? That may not ever happen again. There may be players who play with their kids in the future, but I don't know if they'll ever hit back-to-back home runs." He's right—no father and son have done it since.

I've never been more proud to be a son than watching my dad go out there and play for the Mariners during that stretch. It didn't matter what people said or even if he played well—that was my daddy. All the time we lost growing up, with him being away, all of it was worth it in those six weeks. Because he was there. ◆

KEN GRIFFEY JR.

"I've never been more proud to be a son than watching my dad go out there and play for the Mariners during that stretch."

KEN GRIFFEY JR.

When Roberto Clemente took the field for the Pittsburgh Pirates in the 1971 World Series, millions of baseball fans had never seen him play. But after seven marvelous games, he became a legend.

As notable as Clemente's performance was, it meant even more to his fans in Latin America, who watched the Puerto Rican's slashing hits and spectacular throws with beaming pride. One of them was a 7-year-old boy in Ocumare del Tuy, Venezuela, named Ozzie Guillen—who grew up to play 16 years as a major-league shortstop and manage the 2005 White Sox to the World Series championship.

S O MANY PEOPLE WANT TO REMEMBER Roberto Clemente by how he died. I remember him by how he *lived*.

I never saw Clemente play in person—but I'll never forget his amazing World Series in 1971. You've never seen so much passion in one man playing baseball. Hitting triples, showing off his great arm, he did it all for the world to see. There were some better players than Roberto Clemente, but Roberto had something in him—something in him that shot out of him like fireworks.

I watched it all on TV from my family's house. I was 7 years old. We had an old black-and-white TV, and since it was just about the only one in our neighborhood, around 30 people came over to watch that World Series with us. It was like a Muhammad Ali fight every night.

Clemente just dominated that World Series from start to finish. It didn't matter that he had a real ugly swing—his body going one way, his head going another, and his bat flying around—he still got two hits in both of the first two games. In Game 3, he helped win the game with pure hustle. Leading off the seventh inning, he grounded a pitch back to the Orioles pitcher Mike Cuellar, and he ran so hard to first that Cuellar rushed and made a bad throw. Two batters later, Bob Robertson hit a three-run homer to put the game away for the Pirates.

Clemente got three more hits in Game 4 and another in Game 5. But it was in Game 6 that he really shined—he hit a home run, but it was his triple off Jim Palmer that sticks out in your mind. Just watching Clemente run was an experience. His legs and arms were flying around but he had such determination. Nobody was going to stop him. Nobody.

I still remember that when we watched that World Series, people would get up to get a drink or something, but they'd always come back to watch Clemente hit. You had to watch. We were proud of him.

And what an arm! Clemente just had a bazooka in right field. Everybody remembers the incredible throw he made from deep right field to almost nail Mark Belanger at third in the ninth inning of Game 6. At just 7 years old, I was in awe. I couldn't believe anyone could throw the ball that hard and far and

64

right on the money. I told my mother, "I never thought any human being could do that!" And I remember saying, "I wish one day I can play on the same field that Roberto is playing."

In Game 7, Clemente was still on fire. Cuellar, who was a great pitcher for the Orioles, re-

People talk about Jackie Robinson, but Clemente went through a lot of racism too, being one of the first Latin American stars in the major leagues. He opened a lot of doors for all of us.

That's why I gave my son, Ozzie Jr., the middle name Roberto. I don't want him—or

"Clemente just had a bazooka in right field."

tired the first 11 Pirates, but when Clemente came up, he homered on Cuellar's first pitch, to make it 1–0. The Pirates ended up winning 2–1 to take the World Series. And everyone knew that Clemente was the hero—he got hits in every game and hit .414 overall. You have to remember that back then, people didn't see every ballplayer on ESPN all the time. Many people only saw them in the World Series. And on the greatest stage, Clemente shined so bright. They finally saw what the rest of us in Latin America always knew.

I still remember the day, a little more than a year later, when my father told me that Clemente had died in that plane crash. I cried and cried and cried. I loved him so much—even though he was from Puerto Rico, Latin American kids everywhere looked up to Clemente. It was like he was from Venezuela himself.

anyone else—to forget how special Clemente was to all of us young kids back then. Believe me, if you'd seen him almost single-handedly win that 1971 World Series for the Pirates, you'd never forget either. ◆

Jerry Seinfeld put it best: "I'm making cracks in a nightclub, and this guy was in Game 6!"

An entire generation of New Yorkers followed the ups and downs of Dwight and Darryl, Wally and Mookie, and more as they pounded and partied their way to the 1986 World Series against the Red Sox. But all appeared lost when the Mets found themselves one out away from losing Game 6 and the entire series. Before a comeback that entered baseball— and sitcom—legend, a furious Hernandez left the dugout and walked back to the Mets' clubhouse, figuring the season was over.

I STILL REMEMBER EXACTLY WHAT I SAID: "No way I'm leaving this seat. This chair has *hits* in it."

Only a few minutes before, I'd been the most disconsolate soul in Shea Stadium. It was Game 6 of the World Series, and our great Mets team—which had rampaged through the regular season as the best team in baseball, winning 108 games—was about to lose to the Red Sox. We'd just given up two runs in the top of the tenth to go down 5–3. Wally Backman led off our last chance by popping to left, and then I came up—and flied to center. Way to go, Keith.

At that point I just couldn't watch anymore. Our whole season was petering away and the

Red Sox were about to celebrate on our field. So I trudged back up to our clubhouse, threw my glove in my locker, and slumped in my seat.

I looked down the hall into Davey Johnson's manager's office and saw Darrell Johnson, our top advance scout, sitting there alone. I figured I could commiserate with him —after all, Darrell was the manager of the 1975 Red Sox, who had lost a heartbreaking World Series to the Cincinnati Reds' Big Red Machine. With the game on Davey's TV, we sat and grumbled about what a great year this could have been. "Can you believe this?" we said to each other. Our mood didn't change much when Gary Carter singled to left. We were still pretty much sunk.

68

KEITH HERNANDEZ

"With a cigarette in one hand and a Budweiser in the other, I watched on TV like 50 million other fans."

But then Kevin Mitchell got a base hit to center field, getting our attention. And then Ray Knight singled to center, scoring Carter and making it 5–4. At that point Darrell and I realized that, hey, I should probably run back to the dugout—we might get this thing into more extra innings. But ballplayers are a superstitious lot. We put our socks on the same way every day during a hot streak, we protect our uniform numbers like lions defend their cubs, we eat the same pregame meals. So during a rally like this, I wasn't moving out of that seat. "This chair has *hits* in it," I told Darrell.

"Stay here," he said.

So with a cigarette in one hand and a Budweiser in the other, I watched on TV like 50 million other fans. I watched as Mookie Wilson danced out of the way of Bob Stanley's wild pitch to score Mitchell and tie the score at 5. And then I watched Mookie hit that fateful ground ball to first base, the one that went through Bill Buckner's legs. I watched as Ray Knight scored to give us one of the most thrilling and improbable comebacks in World Series history.

Of course, Darrell and I weren't just watching on TV—we were there, underneath the stands in the clubhouse, and Shea Stadium shook like a Bruce Springsteen concert at the Garden. I thought the whole ballpark might collapse on top of us. The place was just going bananas. A few minutes later the guys came storming through the front door of the clubhouse and I joined the celebration.

Of course we had another game to play—Game 7—but I was never more confident going into a big game. There was no way the Boston players were going to rebound from a loss like that. Even when the Mets fell behind 3–0 in Game 7, we knew we were going to come back and win. And we did—8–5, getting us the World Series championship. What an incredible couple of days.

I do wish I'd been on the bench for that wild rally in Game 6—it was a once-in-a-lifetime moment for everyone involved. But deep in my heart I know that I did the right thing. If I'd gotten up from that chair, no way we would've scored those runs, and you wouldn't be reading this now. ◆

KEITH HERNANDEZ

No player in baseball's long history has ever been more known for his clutch performances than Reggie Jackson. The charismatic slugger helped the Oakland A's win three World Series from 1972 to 1974, and when he signed on with the Yankees just before the 1977 season, he was seen as the Broadway-worthy superstar who could vault New York to the top of the baseball world again.

On October 18, 1977, in Game 6 of the World Series, he came through with the best single October night of any hitter ever. Jackson slammed three home runs on three swings to give the Yankees the championship and Mr. October his lasting legend.

MAN, DID I FEEL GOOD IN BATting practice that day. I was hitting balls into the seats all over the place. I had never swung the bat that good —I was keeping the ball perfectly centered.

My teammate Willie Randolph came up to me by the cage: "Save some of that for the game!" he said.

I'm not sure you can start a World Series game more pumped and confident about your swing than I did in Game 6 in '77. I'd hit a home run on my final swing of the previous game. I'd had a great batting practice. We were one game away from winning the World Series. I really wanted to get after it.

I didn't get to swing my first time up because Burt Hooton walked me on four straight pitches. But I hadn't cooled off at all when I came up in the fourth with the Yankees down 3–2. When Hooton threw a pitch a little up, I smoked a line drive to right. It was slightly off the top of the bat, so I wasn't sure if it would stay high enough long enough to get out. But it cleared the porch. Our 3–2 deficit instantly became Yankees 4, Dodgers 3.

It was 5–3 when I came up the next inning with Randolph on first. Hooton was out of the game by then, and Elias Sosa was on the mound. Sosa threw me a fastball right down Broadway. I like to call those mattress pitches,

REGGIE JACKSON

REGGIE JACKSON

because if you're feeling right you can lay all over 'em. This was the hardest ball I hit that night, a screaming line drive into right. Just like the first one, it stayed up long enough to get out. Yankees 7, Dodgers 3.

We were four innings away from the World Series championship. New York hadn't had one since 1962—an eternity for that franchise dium just went bananas. We were now leading 8–3, three outs away from the championship. I had three home runs on three swings—four straight, if you counted the homer from two days before.

I rounded the bases and went back into the dugout with my celebrating teammates. I wasn't going to come out for a curtain call,

"Stand with your bat on your shoulder and wait for the pitch to get to you. Then you can let loose."

—and the crowd really started to come alive. They started chanting, "Reg-gie! Reg-gie!"

As if I needed a better feeling when I led off the bottom of the eighth, the Dodgers' pitcher was a knuckleballer, Charlie Hough. I always loved hitting knuckleballers. I had learned from my old A's teammate Sal Bando that it really isn't that hard—just stand at the plate and time it. Just stand with your bat on your shoulder and wait for the pitch to get to you. Then you can let loose.

With the crowd going wild all around me, wanting another homer, I took Hough's first knuckle ball and crushed it 500 feet into the black seats in dead center field. Yankee Sta-

but Ray Negron, a young clubhouse attendant who was on the bench, pushed me up the steps, and I took my bow. That ignited them even more.

"Reg-gie! Reg-gie!"

What was going through my head? One big *finally*. It was my first year in New York, on the big stage, and on that incredible night I had earned the city's appreciation and acceptance. I was a true Yankee, one of their own. Finally. ◆

DEREK JETER

Millions of little boys say they're going to grow up to be major-leaguers someday. For a select few, the plan actually comes true. No one followed his own script more than a kid in Kalamazoo named Derek Jeter, who at age 10 marched into his parents' room and told them he was going to be a ballplayer.

I REMEMBER THE EXACT INSTANT I DEcided I was going to be a major-leaguer. It was 1985, the night my mother, father, sister, and I went to Tiger Stadium in Detroit to see the Tigers play the Yankees. Even though I was growing up in Kalamazoo, Michigan, I'd always been a huge Yankees fan. When I played Little League I pretended to be Dave Winfield. So a few days before my eleventh birthday, we went to see a Yankees game.

I was in awe of Tiger Stadium—a big, historic place that even Babe Ruth and Ty Cobb had played in. There were more than 40,000 people there. I couldn't believe all those fans were packed into a ballpark to see these teams. I'd watched games on TV before, but everything looked kind of small. Here, it all looked larger than life. Almost everyone in the seats that day were rooting for the Tigers, but as I sat there underneath my NY cap munching on hot dogs and popcorn, I had my eyes on the Yankees all day. I was really paying attention.

The Yankees lost, 3–1, and I wanted to help them. (I was a shortstop then, too—my dad had been a shortstop and I wanted to be just like him.) I didn't cry or anything when they lost, but I dreamed about someday being out there myself wearing the pinstripes.

We left the stadium and figured out where the visiting players walked to the bus so we could go out there and get autographs. When my hero, Dave Winfield, walked out, I ran up to him and asked him to sign my baseball. He did and gave me one of his great big smiles. What a moment! My little sister, Sharlee, didn't have as much luck with her Tiger souvenir ball. She ran up to Dave a little too late, and by then he was surrounded by fans and he'd jumped into a taxi. She started crying,

DEREK JETER

DEREK JETER

and I didn't make it any easier on her. I said, "He didn't sign your ball because it's a Tiger ball!" She cried even harder, and my dad was like, "Derek, be quiet!"

I kept thinking about the game the rest of the day, how much fun it had been and how much I wanted to be out on the field playing for the Yankees. Right before bedtime I walked into my parents' room to say good night.

"One day," I said very seriously, "you're gonna go to Tiger Stadium to see me play."

I'd said things like that before—all kids do—but this time I really meant it. And they could tell. I'll never forget what they said back to me. They said, "If that's what you want to do and you work hard enough, you can do it." I know that sounds kind of corny, but they really did say that. They didn't chuckle skeptically or warn me about how unlikely my being a major-leaguer was. They always encouraged me. That helped me think it really was possible.

I walked out and went back to my room. I went to sleep that night knowing what I wanted to do with my life. I had great dreams about it. And I'm not sure I've woken up since. ◆

"I dreamed about someday being out there **myself wearing the pinstripes.**"

DEREK JETER

PEDRO MARTINEZ

Joe Torre once said of Pedro Martinez, "He's an artist out there. He's got a baseball instead of a paintbrush."

A sure-fire Hall of Famer, Martinez has always had an aura not just of dominance but of intelligence. Beyond his mastery of pitch patterns—of picking out what pitch the hitter can't handle at that moment—he speaks to teammates and reporters thoughtfully, even poetically, with rich phrases and images.

Martinez makes it easy to forget that half his life ago, he was just an intimidated kid thousands of miles from home, clamoring to learn English just to survive.

I WAS GOING CRAZY. HAVE YOU EVER driven from Salt Lake City, Utah, to Great Falls, Montana? In a beat-up old minor-league bus? When I was 18, I wasn't that into playing cards or listening to music. I wanted to make good use of all that time.

I asked my pitching coach Guy Conti to help teach me English. I wanted to know everything. We would look out the window and read words on the signs as they flew by. It could be anything: *hotel,* or *gasoline,* or *hospital.* Guy would teach me the word, help me spell it, and make me use it in a sentence. And when there weren't many signs to read—those highways are really empty, let me tell you—he would add all the words he thought were important. *Shoe. Notebook. Grandfather.* "What you got for me today?" I'd always ask him as we sat down. He was my dictionary.

I was a hyperactive kid back then. I was spending my first weeks in the U.S. baseball minor leagues. I wanted to reach the major leagues so bad. But since I was a small kid—just 5 foot 10 and 165 pounds—I knew that I would need to use my brain as much as my arm. I just tried to get smarter and smarter.

Education was always important to my family. My parents, Paulino and Leopoldina, always made sure my three brothers and I wore our uniforms to high school back in the

Dominican Republic. (Mom would wash the uniforms every day to make sure they looked right.) When I turned 16 and signed a contract with the Dodgers in 1988 and had to take a 45-minute bus ride every day to go to their academy, I had to do all my homework on the bus. I was almost falling asleep. But I did my homework.

When I came over to the United States, I didn't want to be intimidated by the new country the way some Latin American kids were. I found it fascinating and wanted to take in all of it, but it was so hard at first. Guy was great to me. I wasn't able to express myself, to share my feelings, and he was like a second father to me. (I called him my white daddy.) We would talk about everything. If I hadn't had Guy to teach me things and make me feel more comfortable, I might have just gone home. I didn't talk much at first. But then Guy came up to me and said, "You are going to be all right. I know you miss your mom, I know you miss your country." He was the one who opened his door, he was the one who made me feel confident that I was welcome and I would be able to learn.

When I got to the major leagues with the Dodgers and started to do well with the Expos, yes, I had the fastball and the changeup, but most of all I had a good head. I've always tried to learn from hitters when they're in the box against me. You can pick up things from how they hold the bat, where their feet are, a look in their eyes. You can see what they're expecting and how you can get them out.

That was never more important to me than in the playoffs for Boston in 1999, when I pulled a muscle in the back of my shoulder and was really hurting. Our season was on the line in the fifth and deciding game against Cleveland, but I couldn't start. I was just hurt too bad. But when our pitchers got hit around pretty hard and we were losing 8–7 after the third inning, I knew I had to come in for the team. So I did. I could barely throw my fastball, so I had to think of new patterns for my pitches to get the hitters out—when to throw my changeups and curveballs and where to put them in the strike zone—without them being able to figure it out. I did a pretty good

"My head won that game, not my arm."

job, I guess, because I was able to shut out the Indians the rest of the way. We won the game, 12–8, and the series. But let me tell you, my head won that game, not my arm.

Without intelligence, you don't stand a chance. That's why I'm still so thankful for what Guy Conti did for me so long ago. I still see him every day—he's the bullpen coach for the Mets. Last year I wanted to show how much appreciation I have for him, so I bought him a nice new SUV, just to say thank you.

As he drives down the road in that car, I hope he remembers those long days and nights we spent together on the bus in the Pioneer League. I know I'll never forget. ◆

81

PEDRO MARTINEZ

The 1908 National League pennant race was shaping up to be one of the finest ever when, in late September, the Chicago Cubs played the New York Giants at the Polo Grounds in Manhattan with first place on the line. The two teams played a tight game through the bottom of the ninth, when the Giants pushed across a run for a 2–1 win. Or so they thought.

Fred Merkle, a rookie infielder for the Giants, was leading off first base before the final single; he saw the run score and ran back to the dugout to celebrate without touching second—and he was subsequently called out. Such mayhem ensued that the game was declared a tie and, much to the dismay of poor Fred Merkle and Giants fans everywhere, wound up costing them the pennant. Merkle's Boner, as it became known to posterity, was so immediately infamous that Christy Mathewson, his Giants teammate, came to the distraught rookie's defense in Matty's fine memoir, *Pitching in a Pinch*.

EVERAL NEWSPAPERMEN CALLED September 23, 1908, Merkle Day, because it was on that day he ran straight to the clubhouse from first base, instead of going by way of second, when Al Bridwell whacked out the hit that had apparently won the game from the Cubs. Any other player would have undoubtedly done the same thing under the circumstances, as the custom had been in vogue all around the circuit during the season. It was simply Merkle's misfortune to have been on first base at the critical moment.

Merkle was under the shower bath when the alleged putout was made. Hank O'Day, the umpire, called Merkle out and the score a tie. When the boys heard this in the clubhouse, they laughed, for it didn't seem like a situation to be taken seriously. But it turned out to be one of those things that the farther it goes, the more serious it becomes.

That lamentable event on September 23 seemed to be the turning point in the Giants'

Fred Merkle

CHRISTY MATHEWSON

83

fortunes. A lot of our boys got injured after that. Merkle lost weight and seldom spoke to the other players as the Cubs crept up on us day after day and more men were hurt. He felt that he was responsible for this change in the luck of the club. None of the players felt this way toward him, and many tried to cheer him up, but he was inconsolable.

"Lose me. I'm the jinx," Merkle begged our manager, John McGraw.

"You stick," replied the manager, who makes it a habit to stand by his men.

By the end of the season, when we were tied with the Cubs and had to replay that tied game from September to decide the pennant, Merkle had lost 20 pounds, and his eyes were hollow and his cheeks sunken. The newspapers showed him no mercy, and the fans never failed to criticize and hiss him when he appeared on the field. A lot of men under the same fire would have quit cold.

I was the Giants' starting pitcher for that final game. I felt that my arm was in pretty good condition. But as I started to warm up, the ball refused to break. I couldn't get anything on it. I forgot about the crowd, forgot the fights in the stands, and didn't hear the howling after the game started. I knew only one thing, and that was my curve ball wouldn't break for me.

I didn't have anything on the mound. Merkle was drawn up in the corner of the bench, pulling away from the rest of us as if he had some contagious disease and was quarantined. Once he said: "It was my fault, boys."

No one answered him. Inning after inning, our batters were mowed down by the great pitching of Mordecai Brown, who was never better. As the innings dragged by, the spectators at the Polo Grounds lost heart, and the cowbells ceased to jingle, and the cheering lost its resonant ring. It was now a surly growl.

When the game was finally over, and we'd lost 4–2, it was one glum lot of players in the clubhouse. Merkle came up to McGraw and said: "Mac, I've lost you one pennant. Fire me before I can do any more harm."

"Forget this season and come around next spring," said McGraw. "The newspapers will have forgotten it all then. Goodbye, boys." And he slipped out of the clubhouse. ◆

"By the end of the season . . . Merkle had lost 20 pounds, and his eyes were hollow and his cheeks sunken."

Christy Mathewson

JOE NUXHALL

He was supposed to be pitching against fellow junior high graduates in his hometown of Hamilton, Ohio. Instead, he was staring down Stan Musial.

On June 10, 1944, at age 15, Joe Nuxhall became the youngest major-leaguer of all time. The hard-throwing lefty pitched for the Reds against the Cardinals, and while he gave up five runs in less than an inning, he entered baseball's record books and lore forever. Nuxhall later became a successful big-league pitcher and broadcaster but will always be remembered for his first afternoon, when he traded puberty for a major-league uniform.

"JOE!"

I was in the dugout at Crosley Field, just watching the Reds get beaten up by the Cardinals. I was on the Cincinnati roster, sure, but I never thought I'd get into a game. I was only 15, after all. I'd just finished the ninth grade. I was looking straight at the mound, not paying attention, when the voice called out again—louder this time.

"Nuxhall! Yeah, you!" my manager, Bill McKechnie, yelled. "Go warm up!"

I was so surprised, I grabbed my glove, scrambled up the steps, and . . . fell flat on my face in front of the dadgum dugout! Everybody laughed. But I had reason to be plenty nervous—I was about to become the youngest kid ever to play in a major-league game.

It was pretty bizarre that I was in uniform in the first place. Because so many major-leaguers were serving in World War II, teams were looking everywhere for players. My hometown Reds were scouting my father, Orville, in a Sunday league when they noticed me. I was big for an eighth-grader (6 foot 3 and 190 pounds) and threw really hard. About a year later the Reds offered a deal my parents and I couldn't refuse—$500 to sign a contract, I'd be on the major-league roster but I could stay in school and just go to home games. We said okay. Five hundred dollars was a lot in those days.

On June 10, a Saturday, we were playing the Cardinals and getting pounded, 13–0, in the eighth inning. I loved just sitting in the dugout and watching. But McKechnie decided to see what I had and called on me to pitch. I scooped myself off the dirt after tripping in front of the dugout, warmed up in the bullpen, and made my way out to the mound.

It started okay. I got the first batter to ground out to shortstop. I walked the next guy, and then got an infield pop-up. But then everything went wrong.

I walked the next batter, and up to the plate came Stan Musial, one of the most dangerous hitters of all time. Where I was—pitching in the major leagues at age 15—finally really hit me. This wasn't pitching against 13-year-olds at Wilson Junior High anymore. This was Stan Musial!

Stan rocketed my pitch into right field to score a run, and then I really came apart. All of a sudden I couldn't throw a strike. I walked three straight hitters and threw a wild pitch, and after five runs we were down 18–0. That's when they took me out.

I wasn't happy with how I did, but it was such a whirlwind it was hard to comprehend anyway. None of my family was in the stands to watch me—no one thought I'd ever pitch! So after the game I just walked to the bus sta-

tion alone, paid my 50 cents, and rode back to Hamilton.

Of course I told my parents that I'd gotten into a game, and, boy, were they thrilled. But we didn't have a lot of time to celebrate. Soon, I went to a minor-league team in Birmingham, Alabama, for the summer. And I didn't make it back to the major leagues for another eight years!

I had a pretty good career after that—I won 135 games before I retired in 1966—but I'm always remembered for being the youngest major-leaguer ever, and that's just fine with me. People always ask me about that afternoon, and I enjoy talking about it.

What really sticks in my mind, even to this day, more than 60 years later, is what would have happened if I had gotten the third out of that inning with just the one walk. Would they have given me another shot? Would my confidence have been built up and would I have stuck with the team? Would I have spent my teenage years as a major-league pitcher? It's hard to imagine, but if anyone knows it was possible, it's me. ◆

JOE NUXHALL

"I was
about to
become **the
youngest kid
ever** to play
in a major-
league
game."

JOE NUXHALL

BUCK O'NEIL

**No one ever got as much pure joy from baseball, or exuded it more
passionately, than Buck O'Neil. Throughout his more than seven decades
in the game—as a lifetime .300 hitter in the Negro Leagues, a manager
for the Kansas City Monarchs, a scout and coach for the Cubs, and, most
recently, as baseball's most beloved goodwill ambassador—he adored
sharing stories of the old days with superstars and strangers alike.**

**A wonderful baseball era came to a sad close last October, when
O'Neil died at the age of 94. But only a few months before he passed
away, I helped him capture on paper one of his favorite memories. It's
from 1945, when he found out that baseball, and soon the world, was
changing forever.**

"**G**IVE ME THAT HORN!"
It was late October of 1945, and
I was in the U.S. Navy, stationed in
Subic Bay in the Philippines. My platoon and I
had been asleep in the barracks for about two
hours. Then my commanding officer, a white
man, got on the loudspeaker and bellowed,
"John O'Neil, report to my office immediately."

I was in trouble—I must have done something wrong. But I was about to learn that the
baseball world was doing something incredibly right.

When I got to my commander's office, he
asked me, "Do you know what happened?"

"No, sir."

"Branch Rickey just signed Jackie Robinson to a professional baseball contract. He's
going to play for the Dodgers' minor-league
team in Montreal."

Hallelujah! It had finally happened. I was
so excited, I said, "Give me that horn"—I
grabbed the public-address microphone off
the desk, turned it on, and blasted out to the
entire camp of sleeping soldiers:

*"Now hear this! Now hear this! The Dodgers
just signed Jackie Robinson!"*

You should have heard the hollering! I
woke up the entire camp, about 300 of us, all

BUCK O'NEIL

black men in the still-segregated navy. We whooped and cheered. We even shot out guns in the air. We kept this up for hours—we didn't get much sleep that night. I don't think we made that much noise on V-J Day!

I don't think people can understand how much it meant for Branch Rickey to sign Jackie and finally allow black men to prove their mettle in the major leagues. Before I went into the service in '43 I had been a first

It was progress for America. Halfway around the world, in the Philippines, we knew that this was the first step toward full integration in the United States. We couldn't wait for Jackie to take that first at-bat back home.

And you know what? We weren't the only ones. All the soldiers that night were African American, yes. But my white commanding officer?

He was excited too, right along with us. ◆

"Halfway around the world, in the Philippines, we knew that this was the first step toward full integration in the United States."

baseman for the Kansas City Monarchs of the old Negro Leagues for half a dozen seasons. I even batted .344 in 1940. But I had no chance to play in the majors. All of us—Josh Gibson, Buck Leonard, Oscar Charleston, and dozens more—were shut out.

I had never seen Jackie Robinson play, and most of the soldiers that night in the Philippines had never even heard of him. He wasn't a household name yet. But we were so elated, because this wasn't just progress for baseball.

BUCK O'NEIL

GAYLORD PERRY

On May 31, 1964, the San Francisco Giants and the New York Mets played one of the more bizarre double-headers in history, featuring a 9-inning first game, a 23-inning second game, a triple play, and Willie Mays temporarily playing shortstop. The afternoon stretched out until almost midnight, and the double-header lasted almost 10 hours. But something else happened that will last forever.

"IT'S TIME TO TRY IT OUT."

I remember the moment perfectly. I was on the mound at Shea Stadium, just a middle reliever trying to survive in the big leagues. It was the bottom of the fifteenth inning, and the Mets had just put the winning run at second base. My catcher and good friend Tom Haller could tell I was in trouble. He called a time-out and came to the mound to talk to me.

"Gaylord, it's time to try it out," Tom said. "Let's give 'em something new to look at."

He was right. It was time. I was 25 years old. I was so deep in the Giants' doghouse that I couldn't even see out of it. I needed to have another pitch or I would be a mop-up reliever forever. Or back on the peanut farm in North Carolina.

Lots of pitchers threw the spitball back then. It was part of the game. I'd learned it that spring from a veteran pitcher who'd just joined the Giants. He taught me how to load up the ball—how much moisture you could put on it, where to apply it, how to grip the ball so it wouldn't slip out of your hand, and how to throw it with some control so it wouldn't dive too fast and splish past the catcher. The spitball is kind of like a knuckleball—if you don't throw it right, it'll get up to the hitter looking as big and juicy as a grapefruit.

I also had to learn how to hide what I was doing from the umpires. I practiced in front of a mirror at home. Back then, you could lick your fingers on the mound as long as you wiped them off afterward. Well, I could lick one or two fingers and either wipe off the other ones on my uniform pants or bounce the resin bag in my hand without touching

those fingers. I wanted to be ready for when a game was on the line—like that day against the Mets. This was my career now. I was as serious as a dollar bill.

Tom squatted behind the plate and called for . . . well, we called it the supersinker. Chris Cannizzaro was the hitter. I did my routine: licked my fingers, faked the wipe-off, wound up, and threw. It dived right at Cannizzaro's knees into the dirt—so much that it almost got past Tom for a wild pitch. I threw a few more to Cannizzaro. It was working perfectly, except that the veterans on the Mets picked up on what I was doing. I still remember old Casey Stengel yelling, "Spitter! Spitter!" from the Mets' dugout.

I was learning on the fly and wasn't sure how much to put on the ball, so I ended up walking Cannizzaro. Later, I put so much on that when the hitter, Galen Cisco, bounced the pitch back to me, it was still almost dripping when I threw it to Jim Davenport at sec-

"I loved getting inside batters' heads . . . It was all psychological."

ond base to start a double play to end the inning. Our first baseman, Orlando Cepeda, made sure to roll the ball across the grass back to the mound to dry it off even more. What a teammate!

I threw the supersinker for seven more innings, shutting out the Mets through the twenty-second. It was kind of a blessing that my team didn't score to win the game—I just kept throwing my new pitch over and over, putting up zero after zero and gaining confidence. When the Giants scored two runs in the top of the twenty-third, I was taken out, and we held on to win. It was the first spitball victory of my career.

And not my last. I pitched well enough that summer to become a full-time starter, and two years later I won 21 games and had a 2.99 ERA. I went on to win two Cy Young Awards, passed 300 victories, and made the Hall of Fame.

I don't feel guilty about how I did it. Don't believe for a second that tons of other pitchers weren't doing the same thing. (I had teammates who threw better wet ones than I did.)

I just made it my signature. I loved getting inside batters' heads. I went through my routine of licking my fingers, touching my cap, and all that whether I was throwing the pitch or not. (Sometimes I'd only throw one or two in a game.) It was all psychological. The day before a start, I'd shake hands with the opposing team, my friends over there, and my hand would be full of grease. "Just getting ready for tomorrow night," I'd say.

I loved it. Who would remember Gaylord Perry now if not for this? Priests have asked me whether I threw a spitball. One Christmas, I dressed up like Santa Claus for kids back home, and one of them hopped on my lap and said, "Do you throw a spitball?"

The best was before the All-Star Game in 1969, when the game was in Washington, and Richard Nixon, a huge baseball fan, had all the players over to the White House. When I shook his hand at the reception, he whispered to me, "Gaylord, tell me, where do you get it?"

"Mr. President," I said, "there are some things you just can't tell the people for their own good." ◆

MIKE PIAZZA

Mike Piazza was not a top baseball prospect from the crib on up, like so many major-league stars. In fact, he was only a sixty-second-round draft pick—and was selected by the Dodgers only because his father was friends with the L.A. manager, Tommy Lasorda. Before that, though, his father's connections got him the batting lesson of a lifetime, from the one and only Ted Williams.

I WAS A LUCKY KID. WHILE I GREW UP outside Philadelphia in the 1970s, my father was good friends with Tommy Lasorda, the Dodgers' manager. I got to serve as the team's batboy a few times. But that was nothing compared to a Saturday afternoon when I was 16, when a real-life legend came walking up my front steps.

It was Ted Williams. Ted Williams was at my house! He and my dad had a mutual friend, and he was doing an autograph session nearby, and when he heard I was a high school kid with some potential, he said, "Well, let's go watch him hit!" So he came over to our house, where my dad had constructed a batting cage in our backyard.

I was out practicing when he got there. It was instant awe. I was always a big fan of baseball history and knew all about Ted Wil-liams—the .406 batting average in 1941, his clutch home runs, his perfect swing. He was also my dad's favorite player, even though Joe DiMaggio was Italian. I think it had some-thing to do with Williams being a decorated marine pilot. He was like John Wayne in spikes.

Mr. Williams—I called him that until the day he died—was in his mid-60s then, but he was still a really intimidating guy. He was about 6 foot 3 with this booming voice. I was just a high school kid, not known outside my hometown. And here I was, getting a back-yard batting lesson from the greatest hitter who ever lived.

We loaded up the pitching machine, and I started hitting. He watched about 25 swings before he said, "This kid's really advanced for 16." I couldn't believe it. He showed me a few

things about keeping my head still and tracking the ball with my eyes. I picked up on them right away and started hitting even more line drives. He said he was more impressed with my ability to learn than my ability to hit.

I hit another 25 balls or so while he started telling stories. As if I'm supposed to concentrate with Ted Williams telling stories behind me! He talked about how he was obsessed with hitting .400 that one year, how he played the final double-header and finished at .406. Every now and then he would stop when I hit a rope. I can't repeat what he would say—he was a Hall of Fame swearer too—but I'll never forget what he said when I was done.

"It's guaranteed," he said, "that this kid is going to hit in the big leagues."

I was only a high school kid, for crying out loud—and Ted Williams said I was going to play in the major leagues. That wasn't the last thing he told me, though. As he left the house, he said that hitting in batting practice was only half the battle—that you still have to hit off a pitcher and take into account what he can throw, the count, and the situation. And most of all, you have to take hitting seriously—you

Ted Williams's perfect swing.

"I was only a high school kid, for crying out loud—and Ted Williams said I was going to play in the major leagues."

can't be a nice guy up there. It's not a profession for the light approach. Ever since then, I have taken batting practice as serious business. And when the game starts, I like to think I walk up to the plate with the surliness he taught me that day.

Most of all, though, Ted—excuse me, *Mr. Williams*—taught me to believe in myself. Mike Piazza could someday play in the big leagues, huh? I was euphoric. I felt like he gave me the stamp of approval. Even when I was struggling in college and in my first years of professional baseball, I always remembered that afternoon and the confidence Ted Williams gave me. ◆

MIKE PIAZZA

CAL RIPKEN JR.

ON BEING A STRUGGLING EARL WEAVER ROOKIE

Cal Ripken Jr. made the sports world safe for heroes in September 1995, when he played his 2,131st consecutive game to best Lou Gehrig's legendary record. The Hall of Famer was a Rookie of the Year, two-time Most Valuable Player, World Series champion, and ultimately one of the greatest shortstops ever to play the game. But most people have forgotten that Ripken's stellar career didn't begin that way at all—in his first three months in the big leagues, Cal Ripken batted a shocking .125. How strange, then, that the manager who didn't blow his stack was, amazingly enough . . . Earl Weaver.

LET'S FACE IT, EVERYONE ASSOCIATED with the Orioles in the early 1980s had a healthy fear of Earl Weaver. Especially as a young rookie, you didn't want to get on his bad side. You knew how emotional he was. How he would rip anyone's head off —particularly an umpire he didn't agree with. You see enough replays of this little guy ranting and raving and turning red in the face with anger, and you want to make sure he never, ever gets mad at you.

The day I was called up to the big leagues in August of 1981, Earl sat me down in his office at old Memorial Stadium and told me across his old metal desk, "I'm gonna get you right in there tonight." He wanted me to get my feet

wet right away in a situation that wasn't too pressurized, so he had me pinch-run for Ken Singleton in the twelfth inning of our game against the Royals. I got out there and actually wound up scoring the winning run in front of my new home fans. And two days later, I started for the first time. I played third base and went 0-for-2 against Kansas City. I got my first hit another four days after that.

Playing under Earl really was pressure. My first exposure to him, that spring of 1981, I remember doing ground-ball drills with Doug DeCinces at third. I had a little indecision on one play and Earl jumped my butt. "That right there can *never* happen in a game!" he yelled. "They're *giving* us an out!" He expected you

to execute at a high level. You were afraid to make a mistake.

I hit only .128 during those last two months of 1981—lots of mistakes, considering I was viewed as one of the team's top prospects. But I still earned the starting third-base job the next spring and even hit a home run on Opening Day. Then things went bad. Really, really bad.

In my next 52 at-bats, I got only four hits. But instead of riding me, just when I deserved to get yelled at, Earl did exactly the opposite. He kept putting my name in the lineup and telling me, "Hey, kid, you'll be all right." (Well, he did have a few pointed words: I'd sit down on the bench after striking out, and he'd grumble, "Take the good ones and swing at the bad ones—how the hell is that going to work?") But while everyone was giving me hitting advice—be more aggressive, be more passive, everyone had something for me—he told me not to listen and to trust my instincts. I was just a rookie but he never talked about sending me down to Triple-A. He showed incredible confidence in me.

One day he had me take batting practice with my father, a coach with the Orioles, on the mound. Outside pitches had been giving me trouble, and Dad kept throwing pitches on the outside part of the zone. I noticed the

CAL RIPKEN JR.

pattern and started diving toward the ball a little sooner, and next thing I knew I was pounding those pitches over the wall three or four in a row. It became real easy. Earl was standing behind the cage and he said only one

hadn't been my manager that first month of 1982. People forget how much I struggled. I honestly believe that another manager would have sent me back down to Triple-A, and who knows what would have happened then? I've

"I honestly believe that another manager would have sent me back down to Triple-A, and who knows what would have happened then?"

thing: "Guess you can handle the outside corner." And then he walked away.

I never found out, but I'll bet Earl set this up with Dad beforehand to make me feel better about myself. He cared a lot about his players. He just had a funny way of showing it sometimes.

And, boy, did his trick work. I got hot soon after that and rode it all the way to the end of the season—I finished with a .264 average, 28 home runs, 93 runs batted in, and won the Rookie of the Year award. The next season, I was the American League's Most Valuable Player and we won the World Series.

Looking back now, I have to wonder what my career would have been like if Earl Weaver

seen so many young players who don't have success right away get sent down to the minors and never live up to their potential. How lucky I was to come up under Earl Weaver—a guy who knew the big picture and stuck with me. ◆

Every ballplayer's first major-league at-bat is seared into his mind forever. But that isn't always the most anticipated first of his career.

Alex Rodriguez was only 18 years old when the Seattle Mariners brought him up to the majors on July 8, 1994, to start against the Boston Red Sox at Fenway Park. Getting his first chance at the plate was the fun part. Turning his first double play? Now that was pressure.

MAN, WAS I NERVOUS. I WAS ONLY 18 and had just been called up to the major leagues to be the starting shortstop for the Seattle Mariners. I was only a year removed from my high school prom. It was my first major-league game— and all I wanted was a ball hit to me.

Everyone talks about a player's first major-league at-bat. It's a big deal, of course, and I definitely wasn't happy in the third inning about grounding out to third in mine. But I was more focused on turning my first double play. I really love baseball's fundamentals, doing the little things right, and nothing helps out your team like starting a good double dip. I've actually always felt more pressure in the field than at the plate. You can fail seven out of ten times as a hitter and still be successful. Anybody can strike out at any time. But if you

mess up on defense, everyone notices. So I just wanted to get that first one out of the way . . . and through four innings that day against the Red Sox, I still hadn't gotten a ball. That only made me more antsy.

But I finally got one in the fifth. Lee Tinsley was on first after a single, and then Scott Fletcher, a fast little infielder, smacked one to me at shortstop. It came right at me, which made it even more difficult—it would *really* be bad if I missed it! But also, on a double-play ball, you want to be moving when you grab it. It makes transferring the ball from your glove to your bare hand that much more natural and smooth, and your feet are already moving. So much is made of infielders' hands, but it all starts with the feet. And on this one, my feet were pretty fixed as the ball came right at me.

You have to make a clean catch in order to

106

ALEX RODRIGUEZ

perform a double play. The minute you bobble the ball or make a mistake, you have no chance. Especially with a fast runner like Fletcher up there. I scooped up the ball, shifted my feet toward second base, and fed the ball sidearm to Felix Fermin. After that I was just a spectator. Felix caught it and whipped a perfect strike to first base for the double play. And that was it. *Phew!*

you get in the clubhouse beforehand and how the game is almost secondary.

But nothing makes a shortstop feel more in his element than turning a double play. I let out a big sigh of relief and got ready for the next batter. Good thing I did—Tim Naehring smoked a ball in the hole, and I had to scramble deep onto the outfield grass to get it. I got my glove on the ball, raised the glove up to my

"You can fail seven out of ten times as a hitter and still be successful . . . But if you mess up on defense, everyone notices."

It sounds so routine now, but I was only 18 then. There was a lot of attention on my getting called up, with people debating whether I should be in the big leagues or not. You want to prove you belong. That wasn't hard on the field, where I believed I could play, but off the field it was tough. I couldn't get into bars with my teammates. Heck, my teammate Rich Gossage was 43, more than twice my age. That was probably the most difficult part to adjust to. Playing your first game is memorable, but what you most remember is how people welcomed you, the nervous feeling

bare hand, and heaved the ball as hard as I could toward first. Mike Blowers made a nice pick in the dirt to get the out just before Naehring slammed his foot on the bag. End of inning.

I jogged off the field, feeling like a major-leaguer for the first time. ◆

BABE RUTH

This memory comes from an article that Ruth wrote for the August 1920 issue of *Baseball Magazine*, when he was about halfway through his first season with the Yankees and demolishing his own record with 54 home runs. He couldn't help but recall the first home run of his life—an inside-the-parker, no less—when he was just a troubled child, living at Baltimore's St. Mary's Industrial School for Boys.

I CAN'T RIGHTLY SAY WHICH WERE THE longest home-run drives I ever made. On most of the grounds the papers have come out with stories that home runs I have made were the longest ever seen, but of course you can't take out a tape measure and figure out the feet and inches . . .

None of those drives made any more impression on me than the first home run I ever scored at St. Mary's. I was only a kid, less than 7 years old, and I sure wanted to play ball. They had a team of midgets made up of the smaller kids, and I was after a place on that team.

There was a tall, skinny kid pitching. I have forgotten his name (there were several hundred of us in the school at the time), and he was pretty good for a kid. But I caught one of

his fast ones and drove it far over the right fielder's head, and when I tore around the bases and slid into home plate I was pretty well pleased with myself.

There was never any doubt about my right to play on the team after that, and I graduated from one team to another until I held a place with the one real team of St. Mary's. I might have played there until I was 21, I suppose, and then gone to work making shirts or pressing pants for a living. But instead they got me a job with Jack Dunn's Baltimore team and I made good there.

I seem to have made good on every team I ever played on, and I guess now, if all goes well, I won't have to practice the tailor's trade I learned at St. Mary's. ◆

Babe Ruth (*top left*) as a teenager at St. Mary's.

BABE RUTH

NOLAN RYAN

ON HIS RECORD-BREAKING 383RD STRIKEOUT

Hall of Famer Nolan Ryan is remembered most for his seven no-hitters, blowing hitters away into his mid-40s, and quite possibly owning history's perfect pitching arm. He had scores of memorable performances —yet none compares to the evening of September 27, 1973.

In his last scheduled start of the season, Ryan, then just 26 and only beginning to harness his control, took the mound for the California Angels needing 16 strikeouts to break the season record of 382 held by Sandy Koufax. It ended up being one of the most arduous, thrilling, and ultimately exhausting nights in his spectacular career.

I REMEMBER THINKING IT WAS A LONG shot. It was possible for me to get 16 strikeouts that night against the Twins, but you never figure that's going to happen, even if you try. My manager, Bobby Winkles, and I figured that if I couldn't get to 16 that day, I could come back and start the last day of the season on two days' rest. I gave it all I had—and for a while it looked like it wouldn't be enough.

I was way too pumped up. I came out overthrowing and gave up three runs before getting even one out in the first inning. So even though I wound up getting all three outs on strikeouts, I had already thrown a lot of pitches.

My teammates came back to score three runs themselves in the bottom of the inning, which gave me time to settle down. I got 11 more strikeouts in the next six innings to give me 14 through seven, so it appeared I had a reasonable shot at the record.

I struck out Steve Brye in the eighth inning to tie the record. But during the eighth inning, I strained my right hamstring, and I didn't know how much longer I'd be able to pitch.

I didn't strike out anyone in the top of the ninth, and that's when things really got strange. We were tied with the Twins 4–4, and our fans rooted for us not to score! They booed when Ken Berry led off with a single

"None of the Twins batters wanted to be known as No. 383, so they didn't make it easy."

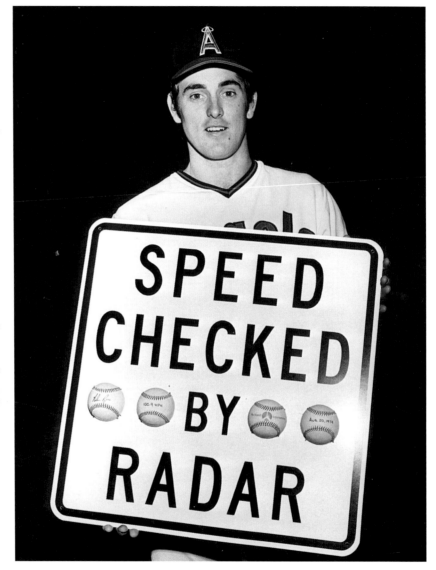

NOLAN RYAN

and cheered when Al Gallagher grounded into a double play. They wanted me to get another chance at the record in extra innings.

I came out for the tenth and got two strikes on a few hitters but couldn't put them away. The crowd groaned when the batters grounded out or popped out. No strikeouts. We didn't score in the bottom half either. I talked with Bobby, and we decided that the eleventh would be my last inning, strikeout or not. I had thrown almost 200 pitches already. So I walked out to the mound for the eleventh not knowing if I would be able to return three days later with my hamstring problem.

None of the Twins batters wanted to be known as No. 383, so they didn't make it easy. Brye grounded to shortstop. I walked Rod Carew, and then something really funny happened. Carew tried to steal, and my catcher, Jeff Torborg, made a great throw to second. If he'd gotten Carew, that would be the second out and I'd have only one more chance. The crowd cheered when Carew was safe on a close play.

Tony Oliva popped to center—some fans were yelling, "Drop it!"—so up came Rich Reese with two out. I knew this could be my last batter—I was either going to finish the season tied with Sandy at 382 or have the record at 383.

Reese struck out on three pitches, chasing a high fastball for strike three. The crowd went crazy. My teammates came out to lead me off the field. I tipped my cap and my night was over. We won when we scored in the bottom of the eleventh, making it all even sweeter.

As I look back now, I have to say this is one of the nights I'm most proud of. This wasn't a no-hitter, but it was a day when things worked out in the end. It was a very up-and-down performance that ended up being a very special game in my career. I still have that record—and a fond memory too! ◆

CURT SCHILLING

ON THE BLOODY SOCK

A Red Sox teammate called it "the guttiest pitching performance in the history of the game." With the Red Sox looking like they would lose to the Evil Empire Yankees yet again in the 2004 American League Championship Series, Curt Schilling ignored the aftereffects of a surgical procedure on his ankle—which oozed blood that millions on television could clearly see—and pitched Boston to a victory that made their eventual World Series championship possible. The Bloody Sock became a symbol of Boston's magical run that no one who saw it will ever forget.

I HAD NO IDEA WHAT WOULD HAPPEN. When I woke up on the morning of October 19, 2004, I knew I was pitching for the Red Sox that night against the Yankees. But I'm not sure I've ever felt more anxiety about a baseball game. I had no idea if I'd do well or if I'd get rocked—again—and let down all of New England in the process.

Every step made me question my ability to pitch. Because the sheath around my right ankle tendon had torn, the tendon snapped back and forth and was really painful. And this was the foot I used to push off from the pitching rubber. I'd gotten pounded against the Yankees in Game 1 of the ALCS the week before—after I'd said I was going to shut up

55,000 New Yorkers—and it looked like pitching again that season was a total long shot.

But the Red Sox team doctor, Bill Morgan, came up with an idea, basically out of desperation. He sutured the ankle skin to some of the tissue covering up the ankle bone to try to keep everything in place. We had to do something because the team was on the brink. We'd lost the first three games of the series to the Yankees, and any loss in the next four games would end our season against our archrivals—again. We won Game 4. We won Game 5. But it would mean nothing if we didn't win Game 6.

I went through my pitch-day schedule as normally as I could—routine is very impor-

CURT SCHILLING

tant to me, and I was doing everything to convince myself that this was just another start. I went to Yankee Stadium five hours before the game, like usual. I met with my catcher Jason Varitek to go over how we'd pitch to all the Yankee hitters. I watched video and then started my stretch routine when I always do, one hour and 40 minutes before game time.

After my stretch, the doctors injected my ankle and foot with painkillers and anti-inflammatories. I remember walking around the clubhouse afterward—you know when your foot falls asleep and it's totally weird to walk, and you can't feel where you're stepping? That's what I felt like, because half of my foot was numb. (And I'm about an hour away from what could be the most important game of my life.) Fifty minutes before game time I went to sit in the dugout for my customary 12 minutes, after which I went out to the bullpen, 38 minutes before the game. (Why 38? It's my uniform number.) I noticed some blood oozing out of my ankle. But I didn't feel any pain, so that was good. During my warm-ups, I had no image of what would happen, how my ankle would hold up under the stress of pitching. I had faith in God that this would work out.

CURT SCHILLING

When the game started, I got some early indications that things were okay. My velocity wasn't up to par, but I was hitting my spots. I threw some good splitters. I had the hitters guessing. My pitches were moving the way they were supposed to. As each inning went by I felt like something special was happening—you can just feel it. It was like an out-of-body experience. I always feed off the crowd's energy, even on the road, but on this night I was so locked in, concentrating so hard, that I didn't even notice the fans. Nothing like that had ever happened to me before. I'd prayed for the strength to compete, not win, and after the start of the game I knew that the Lord had heard me.

During all this, one of the stitches busted, and the blood started really coming through my sock. I knew the tendon was still okay, and that's all I cared about. I just prayed that it would hold out for a while. After the game, people were speculating that the sock thing was staged. People still wonder about it. Well, the sock's in the Hall of Fame—so go test the DNA if you want.

I threw six shutout innings, gave up one run in the seventh, and came out before the eighth with a 4–1 lead. I was totally exhausted —more mentally than physically because of the stakes involved for both my team and New England. I had prayed for strength and gotten it. Some people roll their eyes when I talk about my faith, but it was paramount that day in my life. It was like the Lord took a megaphone and showed me what I was capable of.

We won the game 4–2, thanks to some other guys also—Keith Foulke, Mark Bellhorn —and lived to see the showdown Game 7. We won that, too, thanks to Derek Lowe and Johnny Damon. People remember what I did in Game 6, and I appreciate and am humbled by that. It was an awesome feeling. But you know what? That's what I came to Boston to do. It's what I was *supposed* to do. And for that magical night, the Man Upstairs agreed. ◆

119

Every baseball fan knows that the record for most home runs in a game is four—it's been accomplished by 15 players. But no one hit four homers in a crazier game than Mike Schmidt in April 1976.

On a warm and breezy day at Wrigley Field, Schmidt swatted four long balls to cap an incredible 18–16 comeback win for his Phillies that instantly went down as one of the most memorable individual hitting performances in baseball history.

I WAS IN A FUNK. NOT TOO SERIOUS—IT was early April—but serious enough for my Phillies teammates to think I was pressing. As a young player, the slightest hint of failed hitting mechanics would send me into a panic. I was quiet and jittery.

On April 17, we arrived in Chicago for a series with the Cubs at Wrigley. The first day was unusually calm and warm for April. Before the game, my mentor then, Dick Allen, said that he would help me to simply enjoy that beautiful day's game and not worry about results. For example, after the top of the first I played wide receiver—Dick led me with a long bomb that I caught over my shoulder as I arrived at third for defense. We'd look each other's way and laugh about things between pitches and holler about bad swings by the Cubs, all in an effort to change my frame of mind.

But the game didn't stay fun for long. I popped to center in my first at-bat in the second inning, and then the Cubs started blasting the ball all over the place—after four we were down 13–2. We were so behind that the Cubs' pitcher Rick Reuschel challenged me with no fear in the fifth. I lined a two-run homer into the seats.

As meaningless as it was in the box score at the time, it relaxed me. So much so that two innings later, after we'd closed the gap to 13–6, I hit another homer, a solo shot, to make it 13–7. This was now getting serious. I might get another at-bat with a chance at a

third homer, I thought. Talk about a dream scenario—a third homer helping us come back from 11 runs down?

In the eighth, still down 13–7, we started a monster rally. Dick hit a bases-loaded single to score two. And then Cubs reliever Mike Garman challenged me with a fastball. I smoked it to straightaway center for a three-run home run—my third of the day. But it was still 13–12, Cubs. We were still losing.

And then in the ninth we scored three to take a 15–13 lead. I figured I wouldn't get another at-bat, but who cared? We were about to win one heck of a game. And then, sure enough, the Cubs put up a two-spot in the ninth to send it to extra innings. As I watched, I really felt like a perfect script was being written.

And I was right.

Paul Reuschel, Rick's younger brother,

opened the tenth for the Cubs. Dick drew a walk before my sixth at-bat. I came to the plate 4-for-5 with three home runs and six RBIs—yes, by then I was having fun. And now the game was on the line, and I had a chance

roller-coaster victory. It was that the game sparked us as a team—we won 50 of the next 68 games and ran away with our first N.L. East title. We gained so much confidence and experience over time that we won three more

"Now the game was on the line, and I had a chance to help win it with a fourth straight home run, tying the record for most homers in a game."

to help win it with a fourth straight home run, tying the record for most homers in a game. With a man on first, sometimes the hitter might be asked to bunt. Not this time!

I lined a shot down the left-field line that just cleared the fence for my fourth homer and a 17–15 lead. My teammates were delirious. We scored another to make it 18–15. Of course the Cubs gave us a scare in the bottom of the inning—they scored one and even brought the tying run to the plate—but we finally put them away to win 18–16 in one of the wildest games in history.

The thing I remember most, looking back, wasn't the Dick Allen advice, the four home runs, or even the fun I finally had in the

division crowns and capped that off with the 1980 World Series championship—Philadelphia's first. I honestly believe that 18–16 game changed the course of Phillies history. It will never be forgotten, and, man, it was fun! ◆

123

RED SCHOENDIENST

ON WATCHING ENOS SLAUGHTER'S MAD DASH

Enos Slaughter's Mad Dash around the bases to win the 1946 World Series for the St. Louis Cardinals is probably the most famous base-running play in baseball history. It has been replayed thousands of times in newsreels, highlight videos, and old-timers' memories, but only a few folks can say they witnessed it personally—from inside the Cardinals' dugout. Red Schoendienst, the St. Louis second baseman that afternoon and a fellow Hall of Famer alongside Slaughter, was one of those lucky ones who watched that spectacular play unfold.

I'VE BEEN AROUND BASEBALL FOR A LONG time, about 70 years, and people always ask about the things I've seen. The first one they usually bring up is Enos Slaughter's Mad Dash. It was probably the most exciting play I've ever seen in my 60 years in baseball.

It was Game 7 of the '46 series. We were tied with the Red Sox 3–3 when we came up for the bottom of the eighth. Enos led off with a single, but then two other guys made out. It looked like maybe we'd go to the ninth still deadlocked—one inning to decide the entire season. Talk about tension.

But as Harry Walker went up to the plate, we knew we had a chance. Harry was a good hitter. He didn't have much power, but he could line the ball in the gap pretty good.

That's exactly what happened—at the perfect time.

Enos was stealing on the pitch and got a great jump. Harry lined the ball into left-center, and for some reason the center fielder, Leon Culberson—Dom DiMaggio had injured his ankle a half inning before—kind of hesitated a bit as he threw the ball back to Johnny Pesky at shortstop. Enos just kept on running.

And he could run, boy—Enos was quick on his feet for a short, muscular guy, and he cut the bases very well. A real fundamental player. A lot of guys were faster than him, but he was a darned good base runner.

As the play was going on, I was pretty calm. Why? Because we didn't think Enos was

124

RED SCHOENDIENST

going to try to score! We saw Culberson hesitate and figured Enos was stopping at third. But he wasn't. He was trying to score and win the series for us right there.

Culberson's throw went to Pesky at shortstop. Pesky looked up and was surprised—like the rest of us—to see Enos going home. Nobody had helped Pesky out by yelling that the runner was moving around third. Pesky was shocked. He threw the ball home, and it was up the third-base line just a little bit. Enos slid in safely, and we had the lead, 4–3.

All us Cardinals were watching on the top step of the dugout, but we didn't go crazy. There was still an inning left to play. Enos came back to the bench and just sat down. It wasn't till the game was over that we said, "Nice going, hell of a slide," that kind of stuff. He just sat down and said, "I knew I was going to score."

It was an exciting play, one of the most exciting baseball has ever seen, but I'll tell you, the most exciting play for me was the last out of that ball game, a half inning later. I was playing second base, and the Red Sox put runners on first and third with two out. Tom McBride hit a little squibber off the end of his bat toward me. It looked like it was going to take a bad hop—and of course it did.

I blocked it with my right shoulder, caught

"It was **the hardest play** I ever had to make in my life."

it with my bare hand, and flipped it to Marty Marion. Game over—last out—the Cardinals were the champions. It was the hardest play I ever had to make in my life. It's a good thing I made it—if they had tied the score on that play, no one might ever remember Enos Slaughter's great baserunning. ◆

Red Schoendienst turns a double play.

RED SCHOENDIENST

CHARLES SCHULZ

ON A BASEBALL CHILDHOOD

Charles Schulz, the genius behind the *Peanuts* comic strip for half a century, once called baseball his favorite device. Schulz's bumbling alter ego, Charlie Brown, was disrobed by line drives whizzing past the pitcher's mound. The shortstop, Snoopy, caught ground balls in his mouth and spit them—*ptui!*—to a second baseman carrying a security blanket. Charlie Brown's team lost games by scores of 40–0, 123–0, even 200–0. But we'd never think of booing.

Schulz grew up in St. Paul, Minnesota, very much like Charlie Brown, trying to play baseball but struggling mightily. In a 1995 interview with me, he spoke about how his boyhood spent playing the game forever shaped his love for it.

WE NEVER HAD GOOD PLACES TO play when I was a kid in the 1930s. We would have loved to play on a real baseball diamond, with a real backstop and real bases that didn't move around when you slid into them. But there was no Little League in St. Paul. We did it all on our own. And that's what makes baseball so wonderful—kids can just get together and play.

I was always a pretty good player. I threw very well and could field. But I wasn't a big kid and didn't hit that well. So I never got a chance to play on my school teams.

When I was 15 or 16, I tried out for a real team, in what you'd now call Little League. It was sponsored by LaPlante's Bicycle Shop, which was across the street and around the corner from my dad's barbershop. I rode my bike over there and started throwing with the other kids. Then Mr. LaPlante said, "Go over there and hit a few."

I fouled off the first one and then fouled off the second one. The coaches said, "Okay, bunt one." So I did. They said okay, and that was it. That was my tryout. It was so disillusioning. But that sort of thing happens to kids all the time, in every sport. It happened

to Charlie Brown, of course, in large part because I was channeling what happened to me when I was young.

I did play on ragtag teams that we made up in the neighborhood. We'd find a bunch of kids and just play. One day, when I was about 12, we tried playing against a team of bigger kids. We had no chance. We lost one of

the games 40–0. People thought that Charlie Brown losing games by that kind of score was ridiculous, but believe me, it happens!

I loved using baseball in *Peanuts*. Baseball many. We were waiting to go home. There were lots of guys from Brooklyn and New Jersey, and they decided to get up a softball game. I wanted to play so bad.

"Baseball is the best sport for a cartoon strip, because you don't have too much action."

is the best sport for a cartoon strip, because you don't have too much action. You could never do a basketball or hockey strip because people are moving all over the place. But in baseball, humor can come in between the action. If Charlie Brown made a turnover in a basketball game, he'd immediately have to get back on defense. But if he's pitching and gives up a line drive that sends his shirt and socks flying, there's a chance for reflection and humor. Baseball is perfect because little kids do play it at that age. And they aren't very good at it. But, boy, do they suffer at it.

They say that baseball is a game of failure, but it isn't always sad. Of course it isn't. It's a wonderful game. It actually brought me one of the most flattering moments of my life.

I was in the army in 1945, just after the war ended. I was stationed in a little town in Ger-

And they asked me to. I played catcher—no mask, no protection at all. I stayed very low behind the plate so I wouldn't get hit by all the foul tips. But I loved every minute, just getting to play. I was so flattered that these big guys from New York would ask some unknown guy like me from Minnesota to be on their team.

Isn't that funny? Something as totally meaningless as that, really, in the history of mankind and baseball, a game played in the middle of nowhere and didn't mean a thing, meant so much to me. That's what baseball does for us. ◆

131

OZZIE SMITH

Throughout his entire 19-year career, no player shared his love for baseball quite like Ozzie Smith. The Wizard won 13 straight Gold Gloves at shortstop, making acrobatic plays with one of the most contagious smiles around. Nothing he did during a game, however, compared with the cheers he would get the first and last days of every season, when he would delight crowds with his trademark cartwheel and backflip. They live forever on videotape as a symbol of pure baseball joy.

I T WASN'T MY IDEA. I NEVER WANTED to be looked upon as a hot dog—particularly when I was just a 23-year-old rookie. But it was the last day of the 1978 season, Fan Appreciation Day, and I was coerced into doing it to get the crowd excited.

So on my way out to my position at shortstop, I sprinted and then did a cartwheel into a backflip, high in the air. I kept my glove on my left hand the whole time. I just did it, and the crowd loved it. The team asked me to do it on Opening Day the next year, and next thing you know, I was doing it on Opening Day and the final game of each season. Most people think I did it every day. But it was only twice a year. It was special.

That first year, my teammates had been egging me on to do it for a while. It went all the way back to spring training. We had gotten done running, and since I was a little guy and a rookie, some players were ragging on me that I didn't have any energy left. So I showed them! I did a cartwheel and backflip just to let them know what I had in me. For the rest of the year they said, "You should do it again for the fans."

I'd learned the move as a kid growing up in South Central Los Angeles. I lived across the street from a wood factory. My friends and I would lean planks against the stacks of wood and use them as springboards. We'd take giant inner tubes from truck tires to give us spring. That's really where I learned to tumble. We were flipping into piles of sawdust. I had nerve as a kid, too, so sometimes we'd set this stuff up in front of a chainlink

fence with spikes on it. We used to dare each other: "I bet you can't jump over!" We were only 4 or 5 feet tall. So if you didn't make it, you had problems. But I made it every time.

I never messed it up in the major leagues, either. I did the backflip for 19 years, early on in San Diego and then in St. Louis for the rest of my career. There were a few times when I was injured and wasn't able to do it, so my sons stepped in. O.J. was 6 or 7 and Dustin was 4 or so. O.J. did a round-off backflip, and Dustin did more of a roll. But the crowd cheered louder than ever.

The backflip became something everyone had fun with. It signaled the beginning and end of the baseball season—the excitement of Opening Day and a way to say goodbye. And it was a way for me to express to fans how much I loved to play baseball. It became my trademark, which was great.

I've been retired for a while now, and still, little old ladies come up to me and go, "We know who you are. You're the guy who does the flip!" I sometimes tell them that I played a little baseball too.

I'm in my early 50s now, but I can still do the backflip. I don't get quite as high as I used to. But it keeps my spirits high, that's for sure. ◆

"Most people think I did it every day. But it was only twice a year. It was special."

135

Most people remember Casey Stengel from his managing two New York teams: the juggernaut Yankees from 1949 to 1960 and the laughingstock "Can't Anyone Here Play This Game?" Mets from 1962 to 1965. Few recall that Stengel was once a hotshot rookie for another Gotham club: the Brooklyn Dodgers.

A master storyteller, Stengel sat down many years ago with sportswriter John P. Carmichael to recall his favorite day in the big leagues—and also his first, when he was just a cocksure kid from Missouri looking to make a name for himself.

O N SEPTEMBER 16, 1912, I GOT OFF A train in New York, a brand-new $18 suitcase in one hand and $95 in my pocket. The next day was my greatest in baseball. I was reporting to Brooklyn.

I took an elevated train and streetcar to the old Washington Street grounds at Fifth Avenue and Third. The gate man waved toward the clubhouse. "Go on down there," he said, before he called after me, "You better be good!"

I'll never forget walking into the locker room. There was a craps game going on in one corner. The only fellow who paid attention to me was Zack Wheat. He introduced me around. Nobody shook hands. Some grunted. A few said hello. I walked over to the

game and decided maybe I ought to get in good with the boys by participating in their sport, so I fished out twenty bucks and asked if I could shoot. Somebody said, "Sure," and handed me the dice. I rolled 'em out. A hand reached for my twenty and a voice said, "Craps, busher." I was about to reach for more money when I felt a tap on my shoulder. There was manager Bill Dahlen.

"Are you a crapshooter or a ballplayer, kid?" he asked. I told him I was a player and he said, "Well, get into a suit and on that field while you still have carfare." I hustled, believe me, and I've never touched dice since.

I never expected to play that day. But just as the umpires came out, Dahlen told me, "Get

"I'll never forget **walking into the locker room.**"

in center." Hub Northen, the regular center fielder, had been sick, and I guess they decided they might as well get me over with quick. My first time at bat we had a man on first and Dahlen gave me the bunt sign. The pitch wasn't good and I let it go by. Claude Hendrix, the league's leading pitcher, was working for Pittsburgh, and George Gibson was catching. Hendrix threw another and I singled to right-center. When I got to the bench after the inning, Dahlen stopped me.

"Didn't you see the bunt sign?" he asked. I told him yes but that down south we had the privilege of switching on the next pitch if we wanted to.

"I don't want you to carry too much responsibility, kid," he said, "so I'll run the team, and that way all you'll have to worry about is fielding and hitting." My ears were red when I got out to center field.

I heard somebody holler, and it was Wheat telling me to move back. Hans Wagner was at the plate. He larruped one, and I went way back and grabbed it. In the dugout Wheat said, "Better play deeper for him." But I said to myself, "I can grab anything he can hit!" When Wagner came up again Wheat waved

me back, but I wouldn't go, and *wham!*, old Hans peeled one off. He was roosting on third when I caught up with it.

I did get another three hits that day and stole two bases. When I came up the fifth time we'd knocked Hendrix out and a left-hander was pitching for the Bucs. I was a natural left-handed hitter but Pittsburgh's manager, Fred Clarke, hollered at me, "All right, phenom, let's see you cross over!" I was feeling cocky, so I stepped across the plate, hit right-handed, and got a base on balls!

Two days later we were playing the Cubs when I came to bat for the first time. The Cub catcher, Jimmy Archer, looked up to me and said, "So you're the new Brooklyn star, huh? A base stealer, too, huh? Well, I hope you get on."

I did—and with two out tried to steal. I was 20 feet from the bag when I saw the second baseman, Johnny Evers, with the ball. I tried to slide around him, but no use. He really crowned me with his tag. As I lay there, he said, "I'll stick this ball down your throat if you ever try it again, busher!"

My real education had begun. ◆

138

"Reality has strangled invention," Red Smith wrote afterward, and he was right—for those who witnessed Bobby Thomson's pennant-winning home run at 3:58 P.M. on October 3, 1951, the art of fiction was indeed dead. It might be the single most famous moment in sports history, a flabbergasting turn of events that instantly entered national lore.

Funny thing is, in the minutes leading up to his life-changing swing, the man who would soon be carried off the field in glee figured he'd be remembered only as . . . the goat.

I'D NEVER BEEN MORE DEJECTED IN MY life. I threw my glove in the dugout. My New York Giants and I could feel it —our pennant was slipping away. We weren't good enough to get to the World Series.

And it was my fault! In the final game of the three-game playoff with our archrival Brooklyn Dodgers to decide the National League pennant, I was playing third base, and in the eighth inning didn't make two plays that had really cost us. The Dodgers scored three times to take a 4–1 lead. It didn't matter that the Giants had fought back all summer to force the playoff in one of the greatest pennant races in major-league history. It didn't matter that we'd come so close to the World Series. Our season was just about over. I was beside myself with anger.

But the weirdest thing happened.

In the bottom of the ninth, I was on deck when Whitey Lockman stroked a double to left field that scored a run, making it 4–2 and sending Don Mueller into third. But the next thing I see is Don lying on the ground in pain. I ran out there to him—still with the bat in my hand—because Don was a good friend. I tried to comfort him, but his ankle was badly injured. They carried him off the field on a stretcher, and I was really shaken up. That's when our manager, Leo Durocher, came over and put his arm around me.

"Bobby," he said, "if you ever hit one, *hit one now.*"

What? My mind wasn't on the game at all. I had forgotten that I was now up—with one

140

BOBBY THOMSON

out, us down 4–2, bottom of the ninth, and our season on the line. I thought Leo was crazy. But he was right. I was never the type to talk to myself, but as I walked the 90 feet

back to the plate I started to. "Back to base-ball," I said. "Back to baseball." I was getting myself in the right mindset. By the time I reached home plate I was calling myself an SOB. As in, "Give yourself a chance to hit, you SOB!" That walk back was only 90 feet but felt like it lasted forever.

When I got to the plate and looked out to the mound, there was . . . Ralph Branca.

I hadn't even realized that he'd come into the game. The Dodgers had made a pitching change while Mueller was taken off the field, replacing Don Newcombe with Branca. Now, Branca was no slouch. He was a three-time All-Star and a former 20-game winner. The crowd in the Polo Grounds was going crazy, I'm standing there calling myself an SOB, and . . .

I took the first pitch right down the mid-dle. A fastball right down Broadway! My team-mates wanted to kill me. But I was in my own little world. I snapped out of it for the next pitch and was determined not to let another chance like that pass me by.

Branca wanted to crowd me on the next pitch. He threw it up in the zone and close to my hands. As it came toward me I just got a glimpse of the darned thing. I was fighting for my life up there. I pulled the trigger. I got good wood on it—there's no feeling like hit-

BOBBY THOMSON

ting one really good—and it sailed into the sky. It landed over the wall as I was about halfway to first base.

We'd suddenly won, 5–4, and the Polo for me!—at the nicest place in town. There were at least eight of us, with my mother, several of my sisters, and my brothers-in-law. I think my brother, Jim, got the biggest thrill

"I said, 'For a thousand bucks, the family can wait!'"

Grounds just erupted. I remember kind of hyperventilating as I floated around the bases—I knew what I had done but it was just too amazing to believe. I went around third, came toward home, and made one last big leap onto the plate and into my teammates' arms. Soon enough I was on top of Whitey Lockman's shoulders, and there were people swarming all around us. It was so loud for so long. It was an incredible roar that just lasted and lasted.

It was chaos inside the locker room. When things started to calm down, a representative from the Perry Como radio show offered me $500 to go on the program that night. I said I just wanted to spend the evening with my family on Staten Island. The guy said, "We want you—we'll make it $1,000." I said, "For a thousand bucks, the family can wait!"

So I did the show and afterward drove my car onto the Staten Island Ferry. I did have dinner with my family that night—they waited

out of everything. I still remember how he took me aside at one point.

"Bob," he said. "Do you realize what you just did? Something like this might never, ever happen again."

I thought about what Jim said. It was then, for the first time, that I realized that maybe my home run meant just a little bit more than us simply beating the Dodgers. ◆

143

Joe Torre had an excuse to be at least a little apprehensive. It was his first year managing the Yankees, only months removed from being called Clueless Joe by the ever-understanding New York press. And this was his first World Series, never having reached one as either a player or manager.

But in Game 5 of the 1996 World Series, with his team's season and perhaps—who knows, with George Steinbrenner?—his job on the line, Torre made what he remembers today as the single most difficult decision in his now 25 years of managing.

YOU SHOULD HAVE HEARD WHAT THE fans were yelling at me. I could hear them from inside the dugout. Even down in Atlanta there were some Yankee fans in the stands, and, boy, they let me have it.

"Torre, what the hell are you doing?"

"You're out of your mind!"

I'm leaving out the expletives, but they sure didn't. Most everyone thought I was nuts. Even my wife, Ali, and Andy Pettitte's wife, Laura, were confused up in the stands. They didn't know what was going on either.

"What's he doing?" Laura Pettitte asked Ali. "He's never done this before!"

"I have no idea," Ali said.

Okay, here's the situation: It was the ninth inning of Game 5 of the 1996 World Series. We were tied with the Braves at two wins apiece—so the series was down to a best-of-three—and we were clinging to a 1–0 lead in this game. We had Mariano Duncan on first with two out and Jim Leyritz, our No. 8 hitter, at the plate.

I had Duncan try to steal, figuring he would be either safe and in scoring position or thrown out—which would mean I wouldn't have to decide on whether to get someone to pinch-hit for Pettitte after Leyritz. (We were playing in Atlanta with no designated hitter.) Duncan stole and was safe. But when the Braves walked Leyritz, and I was faced with the textbook decision of removing Andy or

144

JOE TORRE

not, I made the tough choice and sent him up there—a pitcher with almost no hitting experience—despite a great chance at an insurance run and our dominant closer, John Wetteland, out there in the bullpen. When people saw Andy walking up to the plate, they couldn't believe their eyes.

I'm not saying I'm some managerial Einstein, but, hey, I did have my reasons. And I'd been thinking about this situation since the seventh inning.

People forgot who was going to be up for the Braves to lead off the ninth—Chipper Jones, a switch hitter who was much better batting left-handed, and Fred McGriff, a pure lefty. I didn't want Wetteland (a right-hander) to face those guys. I wanted Andy, and since his pitch count wasn't too high, I left him out there. I was willing to sacrifice his at-bat—the whole scoring opportunity—to have him out there in the ninth.

"What do you think?" I asked Don Zimmer, my bench coach. "I want Andy to pitch the ninth."

"Do it!" he said.

Andy popped out to end the inning. Fine.

JOE TORRE

He went out and faced Chipper, and gave up a double. Not fine.

But I was still pretty calm. One, my family had bigger problems—my brother, Frank, was in the hospital in desperate need of a heart transplant. And two, when you're managing land to face the next batter, Luis Polonia. I kind of put our whole season on that matchup right there.

It worked. Polonia hit a line drive to right field that looked like trouble, but Paul O'Neill —who our coach José Cardenal had just told

"I'm not saying I'm some managerial Einstein, but, hey, I did have my reasons."

in the middle of an important game, concentrating and anticipating situations, you don't have time for self-doubt. You have to trust yourself and go with what you think is right. And then don't look back.

When Chipper doubled I did have some reason for concern (I'm not that crazy), but I still thought we'd be okay. Pettitte got McGriff to ground out to first, moving the runner to third. So I brought in Wetteland, just like I'd planned. He got a ground ball to third, so the runner stayed put. Two out. Now Ryan Klesko was up.

I told Wetteland to intentionally walk Klesko. This was about as popular a move as keeping Pettitte in! An unwritten rule is you never put the go-ahead run on, but Klesko mauled right-handers, and I wanted Wette-

to move over a bit into the gap, thank goodness—tracked it down for the final out. We won the game 1–0. And two nights later back in New York we captured the series.

I know in my heart I made the right call to send Pettitte up to the plate, no matter how crazy people thought I was at the time. That game was filled with tough calls—starting Charlie Hayes at third instead of Wade Boggs, walking Klesko, and, heck, I wasn't even going to start Paul O'Neill until Zim changed my mind.

But I made the decision when I started managing, way back in 1977, that I was going to manage in order to win and not worry about answering the questions after the game. Let's just say that after this one, answering those questions was pretty sweet. ◆

ON THE BIRTH OF HIS CRAZY DELIVERY

Not every pitcher's wind-up is honed by mad-scientist pitching coaches in the minor leagues. Sometimes the most distinctive and exotic pitching deliveries are born simply from kids playing ball without a care.

Dontrelle Willis, a 20-game winner for the Florida Marlins in 2005 and one of baseball's most enthusiastic ambassadors, just about dislocates every joint in his body as he slingshots pitches from the mound. It sure helps to get major-leaguers out—but the motion was even better against his childhood neighbors in Alameda, California, when he came up with it just for fun.

MY MOTHER WANTED TO KILL ME. When I was about 10 years old, my friends and I loved to play baseball—and since there were only six or seven of us in the neighborhood, we made up this game called strikeout. We'd all take turns pitching and hitting against each other. There weren't many open fields in Alameda, though, so we played against the side of my family's house. But we needed a strike zone, 'cause you know how kids can argue, right?

So I got a can of red spray paint and painted a rectangle on the side of my house. That was our strike zone. It made perfect sense to us kids at the time. But when my mom came home, boy, was she mad. "Are you crazy?" she said.

But c'mon, Ma. It's not like I spray-painted it on our front door or something!

Man, we loved playing out there. Every afternoon after school, my friends Ross and Reid and a few others and I would go to my house to play strikeout. We played with a tennis ball and just made up the rules. If you hit it on top of the house across the street, it was a home run. If you hit it off the second story, it was a triple. The living room was a double and so on. We improvised and had a blast.

The best part was trying to get each other out—we tried everything. We'd try to throw curveballs and sliders. We'd come up with all sorts of funky deliveries. Me, I was real tall and lanky, so I'd lift my right leg up really,

"I was like Goofy in those Disney cartoons."

really high and have my arms and legs fly around to try to confuse them. I was like Goofy in those Disney cartoons. Then my leg would hit the ground and I'd sling the ball at 'em sidearm. It worked pretty well. We didn't call our game strikeout for nothing!

When I got to high school, I found out that that leg kick and strange delivery worked in real baseball too—not just on the side of our house. I was good enough to get drafted, and when I was 21 the Florida Marlins called me up to the major leagues. People made a big deal about my delivery, and I loved that because it made me remember how proud I was of how I learned the game with my friends back home.

Sometimes, when I'm out on the mound today, I feel the same way I did when I was playing strikeout back in Alameda. It's different because people are watching and counting on you, but I mean the competition, the love for the game. To me, there's nothing better than being competitive. It doesn't necessarily have to be in sports—just being competitive in your work. Going out there and giving it your all and leaving it all on the field is fulfilling no matter if you win or lose. You know that you tried your hardest. If you keep your head up and you take pride in shaking hands with the opposing team, just little

things like that, that's what makes competition so special.

I'm so thankful about how I learned the game as a kid and how I've been able to share my love for baseball as a major-leaguer. I've been back to that old house a few times and looked at that red strike zone I painted as a kid. It's still there—check out the picture on page 149. It's kind of faded but it's still there. It will be with me forever. ◆

DONTRELLE WILLIS

ACKNOWLEDGMENTS

I 'M QUITE CERTAIN THAT BARELY ANYONE reading this page knows how often superstar athletes and celebrities get approached for projects like this and how often they want to help but simply can't. Yet everyone featured between these two covers took time and effort to build *Once Upon a Game,* in large part because of the relationships we've developed over my 15 years in baseball. To all of you, thank you for your trust. Honoring it with this book is more satisfying than you know.

This project would not exist without the help of dozens of others in the game who understood what I was trying to do, embraced it, and helped make it happen. Please bear with me as I thank them all (I hope): Jan Miller, Dave Kaplan, Tom Frechette, Jim Murray and Alan Hendricks, Jeff Freedman and Teal Cannaday, Jeff Idelson, Glenn Geffner, Steve Greenberg, Rob Butcher, Scott Reifert, Steve Fortunato, Ray Negron and Frank Perry, Casey Close, Rick Cerrone, Josh Rawitch, Fernando Cuza, Bob Kendrick, John Maroon, Brian Goldberg, Kirk Dressendorfer and Sherry Clawson, Andy Strasberg, Maury Gostfrand and Chris Romanello, Matt Sosnick and Seth Meehan. An extra-special thanks goes to Jeannie Schulz and Melissa Menta at United Media, two of the best eggs in this basket.

I was simply stunned by how helpful and patient the folks I contacted at various photo houses were, primarily Pat Kelly at the National Baseball Hall of Fame, Marci Brennan at Corbis, Katie Walker at Getty, and Carolyn McGoldrick at AP. You all took what should have been the most vexing part of this project—finding the perfect photographs—and made it a pleasure.

There's no way this book would exist without my two assistants, Michael Groopman and Josh Cooper, who were incredibly helpful and conscientious. Other people who lent a hand in this book's early stages—often without even knowing it—include Kevin Baker, Christina McCormick and Faith Rittenberg, John Thorn, Stan Honda, Andra Roig, Robin Easton, Bill Francis, and Buzz Bissinger. It was also wonderful to get to know and work with Lynne Carey at the Alzheimer's Association, and I truly look forward to having this book—and its upcoming siblings—benefit that noble organization.

Thank you to my editor, Susan Canavan, and my agent, Esther Newberg, for being by my side during the year we worked on this. And the biggest thanks of all goes to my wonderful wife, Laura, who did far more than stand by me during the hardest period—she gave me a baby boy to read this book to someday.

—ALAN SCHWARZ
New York City, December 2006